Eliza Haywood

Twayne's English Authors Series

Bertram H. Davis, Editor

Florida State University

TEAS 411

From Eliza Haywood, The History of Jemmy and Jenny Jessamy *(1785),*
between pages 66 and 67. Reprinted
by permission of Bryn Mawr College Library

Eliza Haywood

By Mary Anne Schofield

St. Bonaventure University

Twayne Publishers • *Boston*

In memory of
Sister Mary Anthony Weinig, SHCJ

Eliza Haywood

Mary Anne Schofield

Copyright © 1985 by G.K. Hall & Company
All Rights Reserved
Published by Twayne Publishers
A Division of G.K. Hall & Company
70 Lincoln Street
Boston, Massachusetts 02111

Book Production by Elizabeth Todesco
Book Design by Barbara Anderson

Printed on permanent/durable acid-free
paper and bound in the United States of
America.

Library of Congress Cataloging in Publication Data

Schofield, Mary Anne.
  Eliza Haywood.

(Twayne's English authors series; TEAS 411)
  Bibliography: p. 129
  Includes index.
  1. Haywood, Eliza Fowler, 1693?–1756—Criticism and
interpretation. I. Title. II. Series.
PR3506.H94S35 1985   823'.5   85–8637
ISBN 0–8057–6913–7

Contents

About the Author

Mary Anne Schofield studied at Rosemont College (A.B., magna cum laude), Bryn Mawr College (M.A.), and the University of Delaware (Ph.D.) and has taught at Villanova University, LaSalle College, Rosemont College, the University of Delaware, and St. Bonaventure University; she is currently a Visiting Associate Professor at the College of William and Mary. Professor Schofield is the author of *Quiet Rebellion: The Fictional Heroines of Eliza Haywood* and the editor of *Four Novels by Eliza Haywood;* she has presented numerous papers on eighteenth-century popular fiction and has published articles in such journals as *English Language Notes, Studies in Eighteenth-Century Culture, Ariel,* and the *Windsor Review.* She co-edited the forthcoming *Fetter'd or Free? British Women Novelists, 1670–1815* and is currently at work on a critical study of eighteenth-century British women novelists and their method of double writing.

Preface

In her preface to *David Simple,* Sarah Fielding remarks, "Perhaps the best excuse that can be made for a woman's venturing to write at all, is that which really produced this book—distress in her circumstances, which she could not so well remove by any other means in her power." Fielding's pecuniary distress is well known and documented (until her death she lived the dependent life of a penniless spinster), and clearly, she was speaking the truth when she noted the financial necessity of her literary career. Charlotte Smith, the divorced mother of twelve children, turned to writing as her only viable means of support, as did Eliza Haywood, Delariviere Manley, Mary Collyer, Mary Davys, Sarah Scott, Elizabeth Inchbald, and Mary Hays. However concerned these women novelists were with financial survival and creature comforts—their professed reasons for writing—their fictions reveal a more important reason for the existence of the British woman novelist in the eighteenth century: the clear necessity of examining and speaking to, of educating other women about their social, political, and economic plight. Their bodkins were happily discarded; pins were metaphorically transformed into biting critiques of the female condition as Fielding, Haywood, Inchbald, and the others turned to the new "woman's work." These novelists felt compelled to communicate truths that male writers apparently did not feel and therefore did not discuss. Woman's work became the "education" of female readers and the necessary production of a feminine literature in contradistinction to the predominant male fiction. Recent scholars have examined women's fiction of the nineteenth and twentieth centuries. Spacks in *The Female Imagination* remarks that women's novels are marked by "subterranean challenges" to male-imposed truths; Heilburn and Stimpson discuss the "presence of absence," the unique coding effect of feminine fiction; while Showalter probes the submerged plots that emerge in feminine fiction. To date, such a revolutionary movement has not been explored in the feminine fiction of the eighteenth century. Here, perhaps, more than in later writing, one can examine this new province of the female. These novelists still feel themselves in the powerful grip of their male forerunners and colleagues, and their works, more than later ones, accurately and devastatingly demonstrate the pure necessity of establishing a feminine rhetoric.

Haywood, like Fielding, Inchbald, Smith, and Jane West, indulges in a sort of parenthetical, palimpsestic, double writing. In each of her many novels, she addresses the problem of women's parallel reality, that "other world" state in which women live, that is relative in all ways to the ostensible reality, the world of men. Haywood is aware that women speak in a subtext, placing their real meaning within the masculinely approved exterior forms. In her novels, she first personally expresses her dissatisfaction with the state of women by subverting the masculine forms to present her own version of the woman's story—the male-created virtue-in-distress theme actually reveals the exploitation and enslavement of women. Second, she teaches her women how to read her double writing. Under the cover of fiction, Haywood anatomizes the eighteenth-century female.

Haywood, although extraordinarily prolific in the novel trade where she exercised her double writing technique, did try her hand at dramas (Chapter 2), translations of continental romances (Chapter 5), and essays, conduct books and moral guides, together with two periodicals (Chapter 9). Her popularity was so great that she even collaborated with Daniel Defoe on the production of the Duncan Campbell Pamphlets (Chapter 4). By and large, however, her fame rests on her novels and romances. Because of their large number, I have divided my discussion into three parts: the early novels, 1724–1729 (Chapters 6 and 7) and the later novels, 1741–1756 (Chapter 8).

Before my own study of Haywood's novels (*Quiet Rebellion: The Fictional Heroines of Eliza Haywood*), there was only George Whicher's 1915 *The Life and Romances of Mrs. Eliza Haywood*. Because of such critical neglect and the difficulty in obtaining access to her works, I have offered extensive summaries of the works in question and have quoted liberally, not only to support my discussion, but to give a true flavor and representation of Haywood's novels. I have used the short titles of the novels in the text proper; complete bibliographic information can be found in the notes to each chapter. The primary bibliography lists the first editions of each work. The spelling, punctuation, and capitalization are a reproduction of Haywood's own.

It is my belief that as the most popular and prolific woman novelist of her age, Eliza Haywood needs to be better known and her works better understood in the twentieth century. She does not deserve to be confined to library oblivion, for her novels and romances form an important part of the popular novel scene of her time. Without a just consideration of her works, together with those of other women novelists, it is extremely difficult to understand the impact of the acknowledged masters of the eighteenth-century novel, Samuel Richardson and Henry Fielding.

Mary Anne Schofield

St. Bonaventure University

Acknowledgments

I would like to thank Nancy Frogsland of the University of Delaware Interlibrary Office; Carolyn Sheey formerly of the Newberry Library; Lynan Reilly and his staff of the University of Pennsylvania's Rare Book Collection; Mrs. Justine of the Edwin Forrest Home; Mary Leahy of the Bryn Mawr College Library Special Collections; and Ann Far and Nancy Coffin of the Princeton University Library staff.

Certainly no work of scholarship is possible without the support and encouragement of one's colleagues, and so, I would also like to thank the English Departments of St. Bonaventure University and The College of William and Mary. Special gratitude is due to Jerry C. Beasley, whose timely advice, assistance, and tact have been most appreciated; to my mother and father, whose constant faith has been my bulwark; and to my dear friends Cecilia Macheski and Deborah Downs-Miers, who have helped me explore the wonders of eighteenth-century British fiction.

Chronology

1727   *The Fruitless Enquiry; The Life of Madam de Villesache;* tr. *Love in its Variety; Philidore and Placentia,* pt. 1; *The Perplex'd Dutchess* (dated 1728).

1728   *The Padlock; The Agreeable Caledonian,* pt. 1; *Irish Artifice,* in *The Female Dunciad;* tr. *The Disguis'd Prince,* pt. 1; *Persecuted Virtue.*

1729   *The Agreeable Caledonian,* pt. 2; *The Fair Hebrew; Frederick, Duke of Brunswick-Lunenburgh* (acted); tr. *The Disguis'd Prince,* pt. 2.

1730   *Love-Letters on all Occasions.*

1732   *Secret Memoirs of the Late Mr. Duncan Campbell.*

1733   *The Opera of Operas* (acted).

1734   Tr. *L'Entretien des Beaux Esprits.*

1736   *Adventures of Eovaai.*

1740   *The Unfortunate Princess* (dated 1741).

1741   *Anti-Pamela,* published by Mrs. Haywood; tr. *The Busy-Body,* published by Mrs. Haywood.

1742   Tr. *The Virtuous Villager.*

1743   *A Present for a Servant Maid.*

1744   *The Fortunate Foundlings;* the *Female Spectator* (published monthly, April 1744 to May 1746).

1746   The *Parrot* (published weekly, 2 August to 4 October).

1748   *Life's Progress through the Passions.*

1749   *Dalinda; Epistles for the Ladies* (dated 1749–50).

1750   *A Letter from H—— G——g, Esq.; The History of Cornelia.*

1751   *The History of Miss Betsy Thoughtless.*

1752   *The History of Jemmy and Jenny Jessamy* (dated 1753).

1753   *Modern Characters.*

1754   *The Invisible Spy.*

1755   *The Wife* (dated 1756).

1756   *The Husband.* Dies on 25 February.

Chapter One

The Life of Eliza Fowler Haywood

Although she was the most prolific novelist-*romanciere* of the early decades of the eighteenth century, with more than sixty novels, romances, and secret histories to her credit, Eliza Fowler Haywood remains a relatively unknown figure in the critical history of the eighteenth-century British novel. It is her own self-imposed secrecy about her life, however, and her failure to leave a written record of her triumphs and failures that account for scholarly neglect. Unlike Aphra Behn (1640–89) and Delariviere Manley (1663–1724), fellow members of the popular "fair Triumvirate of Wit,"[1] Eliza Haywood did not leave a fictionalized account of her life, nor did she permit the true facts of her avant-garde existence to be published.[2] Hidden beneath the guise of her numerous heroines, Eliza Haywood herself remains a mystery.

The few ascertainable facts about her life are quickly told. She was born Eliza Fowler in London, probably in 1693.[3] Her father was a small shopkeeper or hosier, a fact Haywood later suppressed. Contrary to the usual fate of young women, Haywood was educated "more liberal than is ordinarily allowed to Persons of my Sex," as she remarks in the *Female Spectator,* but pertinent details as to where and when have not been found. The next documentable fact is her marriage to the Reverend Valentine Haywood,[4] her senior by fifteen years. The Register of St. Mary Aldermary for 3 December 1711 records the christening of one Charles, "son of Valentine Haywood, clerk, and Elisabeth his wife."[5]

Mr. Haywood held a small living in Norfolk and had recently been appointed lecturer of St. Matthews, Friday Street; whether the cleric resided there or in London, discharging his duties by proxy, is unknown. If he resided in Norfolk, one can imagine the young Eliza rusticating in the countryside with an aging husband and an infant. To a woman educated beyond the usual bounds, such an exile must have been interminable, and one can scarcely wonder at the subsequent events, some unfortunate, of her life.

Abandoning the country for long periods, Haywood unconventionally tried a career on the stage; in 1715 in Dublin, she appeared as Chloe, maid and companion to the courtesan Melissa, in Shadwell's version of *Timon of Athens; or, the Manhater.* The play was not a success, and whether or not Haywood tried other roles in other towns is unknown. Further accounts of her actions in these early years are not recorded. It is not until 1719 with her first novel, *Love in Excess,* that we hear of her again, and after that, not until 1721 when she deserted Valentine Haywood, and the *Post Boy* published the following advertisement:

Whereas Elizabeth Haywood, Wife of the Reverend Mr. Valentine Haywood, eloped from him her Husband on Saturday the 26th of November last past, and went away without his Knowledge and Consent: This is to give Notice to all Persons in general, That if any one shall trust her either with Money or Goods, or if she shall contract Debts of any kind whatsoever, the said Mr. Haywood will not pay the same.[6]

The exact cause or causes of Haywood's flight are unknown; that a high-spirited city girl found country life extremely dull we can assume; that conjugal infelicity and infidelity were the cause we can only imagine. We know only that Eliza Fowler Haywood left her husband on the date noted by him above and that she managed to support herself and her two children through her literary efforts until her death in 1756. After 1721 she had no further contact with Mr. Haywood.

Eliza Haywood was unconventional and opinionated, and she was a gadabout. Preferring the company of other "she-romps" of the period, she set herself up in London. She numbered Richard Savage and Aaron Hill among her friends, and was also included in Steele's circle; his "Sappho," "a fine lady, who writes verses, sings, dances, and can say and do whatever she please[s], without the imputation of any thing that can injure her character" (*Tatler,* nos. 6 and 40), is thought to be Haywood herself. Through such contacts, Haywood developed confidence and was able to succeed on her own.

Recalling her earlier performance as Shadwell's Chloe, Haywood first tried her fortune as an actress, for since the Restoration, the stage had been a source of female employment. Aphra Behn and

Delariviere Manley had both supported themselves early in their careers by their dramatic efforts. Although both women were more skilled as playwrights than as actresses, they finally resorted to novel writing as a more steady and secure source of income. Haywood's success on the stage was limited, too, and she quickly turned to playwriting as a more certain means of earning a living. On 4, 5, and 6 March 1721, her tragedy, *The Fair Captive,* was acted at Lincoln Inn Fields. One other performance, on 16 November was given for the author's benefit, and then *The Fair Captive* was allowed to die gracefully. Spasmodically, during the early years of her career, Haywood would compose a play; in 1723, the comedy, *A Wife to be Lett;* in 1729, the tragedy, *Frederick, Duke of Brunswick-Lunenburgh;* and in 1733 an adaptation of Fielding's *Tragedy of Tragedies; or, the Life and Death of Tom Thumb the Great,* renamed *The Opera of Operas,* and written in conjunction with author-playwright William Hatchett. By and large, however, the stage never offered the attraction (or the money and fame) that Haywood was able to find as a novelist and *romanciere*. As she characteristically noted, "The stage not answering my Expectation, and the averseness of my Relations to it, has made me Turn my Genius another Way; I have printed some Little things which have mett a Better Reception then they Deserved, or I Expected: and have now Ventur'd on a Translation to be done by Subscription."[7]

The subscription printing to which she refers concerned her translation of *Letters from a Lady of Quality to a Chevalier* (1720, dated 1721), purportedly written by "the Famous Monsieur Pursault." Capitalizing on the continental vogue of romance, she found a ready, avid English audience for her amorous and often licentious tales. Her *Letters from a Lady of Quality,* a rather loose translation of *Lettres nouvelles. . . . avec frieze lettres amoureuses d'une dame à un cavalier,* a work patterned on the famous *Portuguese Letters,* is an early yet penetrating psychological portrait of the female psyche. The author of the letters, obviously a woman of quality, displays a wide range of emotions as she is courted, scorned, and courted again by her lover. Such a deep examination of the consciousness of the female sets the pattern for the majority of Haywood's later works. Although never again treated with such blatant psychological force as in these *Letters,* Haywood's heroines wrestled with the same female problems of exploitation, discrimination, and the like in her subsequent novels and romances.

Like the fictional lady of quality, Haywood, too, was courted and then scorned by her public. Abandoning the theatre, she won the adoration of the public with her first novel, *Love in Excess; or, The Fatal Enquiry* (1719), which was so successful that it went through five separate editions before being included in the 1724, four-volume *The Works of Mrs. Eliza Haywood;* it provided the model for Haywood's future romances. Always writing of love in excess, Haywood became best known for her works of passionate intrigue and amorous, often titillating, adventure. For example, in 1724 alone she composed no fewer than ten original romances. Her bookseller, William Rufus Chetwood, together with Daniel Browne, Jr. and Samuel Chapman, were chiefly responsible for Haywood's rocketing popularity. They seemed always ready to provide her ever-increasing reading public with her latest novel, published in octavo size for the price of one to three shillings. At such prices, Haywood was writing neither for the poor nor the rich—her audience was solidly middle-class women.[8]

Haywood, the New Reading Public, and the Woman Question

During the early decades of the eighteenth century, the English reading public was undergoing a definite change. Women especially were coming to have a voice in the kinds of books written and published, and by 1740 they witnessed the founding of the first circulating library. The sudden burgeoning of novel reading reflected the increased leisure time available to them. Ian Watt observes in *The Rise of the Novel,* "Women of the upper and middle classes could partake in few of the activities of their menfolk, whether of business or pleasure. It was not usual for them to engage in politics, business or the administration of their estates, while the main masculine leisure pursuits such as hunting and drinking were also barred. Such women, therefore, had a great deal of leisure, and this leisure was often occupied by omnivorous reading."[9] Romances and novels provided the vicarious excitement and liberating fantasies for which these readers yearned. Contemporary events and people, together with fictionalized romance heroes and heroines, dominated the popular literary scene and provided readers with the much sought-after escape. As Jerry C. Beasley notes, "What the average reader of the [1720s], 1730s and 1740s really wanted was an entertaining, ethically authoritative narrative literature that translated heroism into immediate contemporary terms."[10]

What women wanted to read and believe was that their dull, despairing lives, which enslaved them to men legally, financially, and intellectually, were actually the testing grounds of extraordinary heroism.

Since the majority of the popular romances and novels focused on the struggle between a sexually aggressive male victimizer and his victim, the equally submissive and quiescent female, a person with twentieth-century sensibility appropriately feels that what is at issue is a struggle for power. As women, especially middle-class women, were phased out of the economic marketplace because of increasing industrialization and urbanization, they were made to assume a steadily diminishing role in the real world of men; forced out of production centers, they moved further and further into a pretend world of romantic love and fantasy relationships. The popular novelists, certainly Haywood among them, articulated this new preserve of the fashionable, well-to-do, but unnecessary female. Factors of more free time, less work, and the emotional need to be wanted combined with women's increasing literary skills to create and support this milieu of the popular novelist. Men in their lives and in their literary works relegated women to sex objects, leisure-time playthings; popular feminine novelists alluded to and used, yet countered the imprisoning manmade fictions.

Specifically, the majority of women writers of the eighteenth century engaged in a process of double writing. Not content merely to adopt a masquerade technique in terms of their female protagonists, these novelists used the cover story of their romance plots to mask their feminist, aggressive intentions and to expose as facile and utterly fatuous the fictions created by men. Almost without exception, the plot of these numerous works details and describes the state of the divided heroine. Outwardly forced to submit to male dominance and control, inwardly she aggressively rebels and creates elaborate strategems that attempt to avoid such exploitation. These novelists created submerged meanings, meanings hidden within or behind the more accessible public content of their work. This process can be viewed as one of aggressive deplacement; their invented characters act out what cannot, in fact, take place.

Barbara Bellow Watson in her article, "On Power and the Literary Text," explores this feminine process of double writing and double reading as she reveals the power struggle inherent in being female in the male-dominated world. On the surface, she notes, the weaker sex must accommodate itself to the stronger sex:

The most essential form of accommodation for the weak [the female] is to conceal what power they do have and to avoid anything that looks like threat or competition. Therefore we must not expect . . . the literature written by women . . . to tell us much about so sensitive a topic in the form of declarations, manifestos, plot summaries, or even broad outlines of characterization. We begin instead to look at such techniques as ambiguity, equivocation, and expressive symbolic structure.[11]

The female novelist adopts what Nancy K. Miller has labeled a "posture of imposture"[12] in an attempt to delineate adequately the true state of being female; these novelists learned to place their real meanings in a parenthetical, subtextual level.[13] Their rhetoric was paradoxical at best, for their works were read on the surface primarily for escape, not entrapment. Ironically, however, the more the woman reader was led to escape into the romantic fictional world, the more she actually was led into and entrapped by the parallel reality played out in the subtext of the novels. Dreams, fairy tales, fables, and visions avidly displayed this psychological reality that the subtext addressed. The point is that the female novelist entrapped her unsuspecting readers first by presenting the escape tale they expected and desired, and then, under the cover of her fiction, revealed to them their de facto imprisoned and exploited state.

Haywood was a pioneer of the new style. Later novelists such as Sarah Fielding, Elizabeth Inchbald, and Jane West employed this same technique of double writing that reached its eighteenth-century culmination in the novels of Jane Austen. Virginia Woolf, with her own brand of covert and overt fiction, writes, "Jane Austen is thus a mistress of much deeper emotion than appears upon the surface. She stimulates us to supply what is not there. What she offers is, apparently, a trifle, yet is composed of something that expands in the readers' mind and endows with the most enduring form of life scenes which are outwardly trivial . . . . Here, indeed, in this unfinished and in the main inferior story, are all elements of Jane Austen's greatness."[14] This exterior triviality countered by an interior expansion (what Woolf notes as the hallmark of Austen's technique) is also the rhetorical strategy employed by the majority of those earlier popular female novelists, especially Eliza Haywood.

The Scandal Novels and Her Later Years

Haywood occasionally attempted other kinds of writing. Riding the wave of Delariviere Manley's popular *The New Atalantis* (1709), she produced her own scandal novels or romans à clef, the best of which were *Memoirs of a Certain Island Adjacent to the Kingdom of Utopia* (1725–26) and *The Present Intrigues of the Court of Carimania* (1726). Perhaps they were too good, for they evoked great public clamor, much of it fed by Alexander Pope. In the cause of righteous zeal for public morality (and for a fancied insult), he heaped abuse on Haywood and these works in his 1728 *The Dunciad*. Apparently crushed by Pope's castigation, Haywood was silenced temporarily, and, after the 1736 publication of *The Adventures of Eovaai*, she published nothing for six years.

When she did reappear, it was as the sober champion of the status quo and writer of domestic fiction. Gone are the racy heroine and the equally captivating author of the novels of the early period; instead of the exotic Lasselia or Idalia, the reader is presented with mundane Betsy Thoughtless or Jenny Jessamy. These novels of her later period are better constructed and more fully developed, but they lack the rush of passion and the joie de vivre of the early works. Betsy Thoughtless marries Mr. Trueworth, to be sure, and Jenny gets her Jemmy, but the reader gets tedious sermons and moral lessons.

These fictionalized sermons grew out of the popularity of conduct books and moral guides. During her six-year silence, Haywood tried her hand at publishing; not only did she print *The Busy-body* and *Anti-Pamela* at the "Sign of Fame in Covent Garden," she attempted moral guides in the guise of *The Fortunate Foundlings*, and in the two novels attributed to her, *Dalinda* and *The History of Cornelia*. Her later years were tinged with tones of quasi-repentance and moral instruction; though forced to present her works anonymously after *The Dunciad* attack, Haywood did survive for the next fourteen years. She herself provides the most fitting self-portrait of her later years in the *Female Spectator* when she writes:

I have run through as many Scenes of Vanity and Folly as the greatest Coquet of them all. —Dress, Equipage, and Flattery were the Idols of my Heart.—I should have thought the Day lost, which did not present me with some new Opportunity of shewing myself.—My Life, for some

Years, was a continued Round of what I then called Pleasure, and my whole Time engross'd by a Hurry of promiscuous Diversions.—But whatever Inconveniences such a manner of Conduct has brought upon myself, I have this Consolation, to think that the Publick may reap some Benefit from it:—The Company I kept was not, indeed, always so well chosen as it ought to have been, for the sake of my own Interest or Reputation; but then it was general, and by consequence furnished me, not only with the Knowledge of many Occurrences, which otherwise I had been ignorant of, but also enabled me . . . to judge of the various Passions of the Human Mind, and distinguish those imperceptible Degrees by which they become Masters of the Heart, and attain Dominion over Reason.

With this Experience, added to a Genius tolerably extensive, and an Education more liberal than is ordinarily allowed to Persons of my Sex, I flatter'd myself that it might be in my Power to be in some measure both useful and entertaining to the Publick. [15]

Haywood's career, divided between her role as "arbitress of passion" and that of stern moralizer, is emblematic of the eighteenth century. The age was one of contradictions and dialectics. At first glance, the Age of Reason seems to project an image of tranquility, but one has only to look at Hogarth's prints to know that this serenity was threatened by the dark and disruptive facts of crime, poverty, and human misery. Although the great literature of the Augustan age was marked by reason and good sense, we know from *Gulliver's Travels* and *The Dunciad* that Swift and Pope worried profoundly about the challenges to their moral and aesthetic values posed by a changing social order and an emerging popular culture.

The polarities of the age are the polarities of Haywood: there is frankly brutal sexual exploitation in her early novels of the 1720s and 1730s contrasted with the moral refinement and sententiousness in the works of the 1740s and 1750s. Most of the novels of her first period depict the troubled heroine who is unable to reconcile contradictory elements within herself and accept her position in society; she is unwilling to be a mere sexual plaything and yet is unable fully to assert herself. Unable to be independent and aggressive while appearing docile and submissive, she ends her struggle in exile or death. The later novels offer a more conservative portrait of the virtuous heroine who is tested throughout the story, but remains true to her virtue and her womanly position and is rewarded with marital bliss. This woman, it would appear, has learned Miller's "posture of imposture" and can adapt herself to the exterior role defined for her by the male and live her interior life in a way that admits to her true self. No longer mirrored in Hogarth's engravings, these later works suggest a Reynolds or Gainsborough portrait. The earlier rebellious flare is followed by a more conservative, less risky portrayal.

As a member of a small yet select group of writers challenging the status quo, Haywood is an important figure in the minor fiction of her age. Certainly as the most prolific novelist, male or female, of the eighteenth century, she deserves critical attention; more important, her place among the early feminists as a writer sensitive to the position of the eighteenth-century woman needs more examination and better understanding. Determined not to acquiesce quietly in male-imposed patterns and rules, and unwilling to see women remain in an inferior position, Haywood challenged such complacency and offered new alternatives of viewing the feminine self. Her works should not be relegated to literary history's wastebin as quaint examples of the fictional development of a bygone era; instead, they must be read and reevaluated as statements of the leading voice in the feminine movement that has its roots in her time.

Chapter Two
Haywood as Dramatist

Haywood did not begin her literary career as a rebel. Although she presented a mutinous face to ordered society when leaving her husband, her first fully independent venture was strictly in keeping with earlier feminist actions. Aphra Behn, Delariviere Manley, and Susanna Centlivre had demonstrated that independent women could have successful, self-sufficient careers in the theatre. Haywood's first appearance as a "femme sole" was as an actress in Shadwell's revival version of *Timon of Athens* (1715), but her performance was a dismal failure, and she turned to playwriting as an alternative means of support. It was natural for her to do so, for her role models, Behn and Manley, although best known as novelists, had begun their own careers as dramatists, and Behn's plays were still produced during Haywood's early years.

The Fair Captive

Haywood's first play, *The Fair Captive* (1721),[1] introduces the archetype of virtue in distress—Brave Alphonso must redeem his "Captive Mistress," Isabella. The sexual fantasy is well established, for not only is the female captive in the male imagination, she is physically imprisoned within the seraglio walls.

The play opens with the Spaniard, Alphonso, arriving at Constantinople, an "Earthly Paradise" (p. 1), which he says is "The Beauteous Mistress of the *Eastern* World" (p. 2). But like the woman, who in "Spite of her Pomp, she drooping, still laments / Her ravish'd Freedom, and her lost Estate" (p. 2), Constantinople has been rifled of all her charms; Thracians, Huns, Saracens, Goths, and most recently, the "barbarous Scythian crew" (p. 2) have plundered and raped her. The city as an image of violation is a timely metaphor of the female condition.

Alphonso has come to rescue another violated object, his Isabella, "That lovely Maid, that dear, that heavenly Fair! The brightest Soul that ever was infus'd / Into an Angel's Frame" (p. 2). Imprisoned in the seraglio, "Guards of Eunuchs watch her every Motion" (p. 4). Although the exploits of Alphonso and Isabella form the main plot line, Haywood tells several other stories in an effort to portray the all-encompassing effects of female enslavement. Thus Irene, the Visier's wife, who says she is able to "see the Villain thro the fawning courtier" (p. 16), is plotting her "just Revenge" (p. 7) on her husband, who has been unfaithful to her yet again. Simultaneously, the play tells of Daraxa's revenge, also on the Visier for seducing and then abandoning her. Mustapha, the Grand Visier, "a Slave to love" (p. 13), meanwhile is enamored of Isabella and tries to arrange an assignation with her. Irene has managed to contravene his orders and arranges for Isabella to be sent back to Spain. But the Visier, with the help of Achmat and Hally, yes-men of the court, upsets her plans and apprehends Alphonso in the seraglio, where Daraxa has obtained entrance for him. Unable to make her revenge work, in her despair Daraxa stabs herself in front of the Visier. The Visier is shocked and says, "I seem a Monster even to myself " (p. 39), but he does not cease plotting and planning how he will "enjoy" Isabella. Nothing it seems can stop him.

Even at this early date, Haywood's rage is evident, as through her character of Irene she tries to control the tyrannical male. Disguised, Irene sees her plot with Isabella hatch but then misfire; Irene is stabbed by mistake and dies. In the midst of the melee, Isabella escapes. Great confusion follows. Alphonso accuses her of being unfaithful, but the Visier's dying words exonerate her, and the lovers are united at the end.

The Fair Captive is about love and all the distortions, hypocrisies, and frauds that result from yielding to an untempered, unbalanced passion. Although only Alphonso openly admits that he is controlled by passion, Mustapha, Irene, Daraxa, and Isabella obviously are as well. What Haywood has provided is a graduated look at love: Alphonso and Isabella's is pure; the Visier's is rape centered; Daraxa's is revengeful; and Irene's is foolish and pride oriented. Subplots also involve perversions of love: Oxmia and Achmat desire power so that they can get rid of the Visier; Hally also is consumed by thoughts of power. Ultimately, pure love, the balanced approach of reason and passion, triumphs.

In this work, Haywood examines what happens when, without rational control, truth has to go into hiding; when reality is covered over and only the appearance of things is visible. She has not yet begun to place her coded message, the double plot, in the secondary story line; there is no posture of imposture. Instead, she openly exposes women's subjugation, exploiting this condition by setting the tale in a seraglio, and portraying the villain as lustful and virgin-hungry.

Haywood is, however, still concerned with fictional standards and does write a happily-ever-after ending for the hero and heroine; she is unwilling at this early date to jeopardize the success of the overt story with covert teaching. When one examines this first work closely, however, her discontent is evident. The extraordinary complications of the plot entrap and fetter not only the female characters, but the female readers. All are caught in the webs that the male so treacherously and effortlessly weaves. As Haywood succinctly yet powerfully notes in the epilogue:

> All Women, there, obey—because they must.
> Silent, they sit, in passive Rows, all Day;
> And musing, cross-legg'd, stitch strange Thoughts away.
> Provoking Life!—stew'd up like Ponds of Fish,
> They feed, fatten, for one Glutton's [Dish]! . . .
> Dreadful Reflections!—Call they this a Wife?
> 'Tis an unwholesome, dull—unactive Life!

The Fair Captive is a frontispiece for Haywood's entire corpus.

A Wife To be Lett

Her next play, the comedy *A Wife To be Lett* written in 1723,[2] was acted at the Drury Lane Theatre three times beginning August 12 of that year. Because of the indisposition of one of the actresses, Haywood herself took the part of the wife, Mrs. Graspall, and the moderate success of the play was apparently due to her appearance. By 1723 she was successful as a novelist, and Londoners were anxious to see the hyena in petticoats who had taken the popular novel scene by storm. The Prologue, spoken by Theophilus Cibber, makes her position clear:

> A dangerous *Woman-Poet* wrote the Play:
> One, who not fears your Fury, tho' prevailing,
> More than your Match, in everything, but Railing.
> Give her fair Quarter, and whene'er she tries ye,

> Safe in superior *Spirit,* she defies ye:
> Measure her Force, by her *known Novels,* writ
> With manly Vigour, and with Woman's Wit.

Haywood's wit patterns this play along typical Restoration comedy lines. Courtly is in love with Marilla, the niece of the money-loving Mr. Fairman, but unfortunately, she is pledged to Toywell "the greatest fop in nature" (p. 8), "who has no Sense of what is truly valuable, and esteems *Marilla* only for her Fortune" (p. 8). His confidante, Captain Gaylove, has a plan, however; he will introduce Courtly to another beauty, Celemena, and hope to divert his affections. Of course, it is only a momentary interest, for Courtly is a genuine lover, and although he is rewarded with Marilla at the conclusion, it is not before he has endured a long and complicated test. Likewise, Celemena loves Courtly but is betrothed to Sneaksby by her father because he wants Sneaksby's money. Celemena is subject to great persecution before she is allowed to live happily ever after. Her father tells her that Sneaksby is "good-natur'd . . . and rich; two things a young Woman ought to prefer to a full Head and light Purse" (p. 22). Celemena is shocked, but though "Duty obliges me not to dispute with your Commands . . . I may find some way to evade 'em" (p. 22). She will revolt. Marilla and Celemena are examples of the unmarried, exploited female. Mrs. Graspall, describing her "uncoveted condition" (p. 13) of being a wife, clarifies the unhealthy position of married women: "O! to what Fate are wretched Women born! Condemn'd to Slavery, tho' conscious of superior Merit, and bound to obey the severe Dictates of a very Fool, when e'er the Name of Husband gives 'em Force" (p. 13). She turns the tables on her husband, however, and manages to control his plan, thus reducing to total absurdity the notion of female obedience when she agrees to be "sold" by her husband to Sir Harry; instead, she takes the money and gives it to Gaylove.

Like *The Fair Captive, A Wife To be Lett* introduces the themes, image patterns, metaphoric complexes, and authorial anger that will be found in Haywood's mature work. *A Wife To be Lett* concerns itself with exploitation and enslavement, but here more of Haywood's mature style is evident as she creates women characters who are unafraid to act on behalf of their own fate. They take matters into their own hands and arrange affairs so that, like Marilla and Celemena, for example, they get the husbands they have chosen, not those parentally selected for them. Like Mrs. Graspall, subversively, yet effectively, the women make their presence known.

Frederick, Duke of Brunswick-Lunenburgh

In 1729 Haywood tried her hand at a tragedy, *Frederick, Duke of Brunswick-Lunenburgh,*[3] which was first produced at Lincoln's Inn Fields on 4 March 1729. During the six years between *A Wife To be Lett* and *Frederick,* she had learned to tighten up the plot and structure of her plays. Instead of the plethora of incidents that made her first two plays action packed if sometimes unintelligible, however, *Frederick* suffers from dull, platitudinous conversations that retard the action.

As the play begins, Frederick, who was patterned after Frederick Lewis, Prince of Wales, has just been crowned Duke of Brunswick-Lunenburgh. Unfortunately, Count Waldec is not pleased with this turn of events and has begun to plot against Frederick. Adelaid, Waldec's sister, is also set to have revenge on Frederick, although she is very much in love with him. Even though he abandoned her in order to marry a Saxon princess, two years later, Adelaid still "struggles with the galling Chains; / A Slave she is, and still a Slave remains" (p. 11); and, although pursued by the Duke of Wirtemberg, she still cares only for Frederick. Waldec wants to destroy the Duke so he can reclaim his forfeited fortune, the illegal bounty from his relationship with an enemy of the Duke's. He counsels his sister that she must now consent to marry Wirtemberg in order to aid his plan. But Adelaid continues to be blinded and enslaved by her love for Frederick—her "Passion's deaf to Reason" (p. 10)—and rather than have Wirtemberg, she will "forsake this busy World, / And in a Cloyster's silent, safe Recess / Pass the Remainder of my Days" (p. 23).

Waldec is still bent on revenge; he tells Wirtemberg that Frederick has already deflowered Adelaid. Having thus convinced the faithful Wirtemberg of Frederick's essential evilness, Waldec and his friend Ridolpho hope that Wirtemberg, in his rage, will kill Frederick for them. Their plans, however, are thwarted when Adelaid overhears their scheme and warns Frederick. A fight ensues. Ridolpho and Waldec are slain, but not before Frederick, now fully forgiven by Wirtemberg, who has learned the truth, is killed by Waldec. Wirtemberg alone is left to praise the Duke's greatness.

Frederick, Duke of Brunswick-Lunenburgh is a bombastic attempt to model a work on the heroic drama of the period. Although Frederick, Wirtemberg, and Adelaid are presented in a sympathetic mode, much of their rhetoric makes them look just silly. The plot basically hinges on the revenge of the jilted woman, and very little is concerned with the woman question that was to interest Haywood so much in her later novels. This play is an exercise in writing tragedy and nothing more.

The Opera of Operas

In conjunction with actor-playwright William Hatchett, Haywood tried for the last time to produce a successful piece for the theatre; in 1733 they rewrote Fielding's *Tragedy of Tragedies; or, the Life and Death of Tom Thumb the Great.* Modeled on Gay's *The Beggar's Opera,* their work, *The Opera of Operas,*[4] is a hybrid concoction of song and dance, bombastic speeches, and pithy remarks that does manage to include several typical Haywood themes and image patterns.

The play is based on the love of tiny Tom Thumb for the King's daughter, Huncamunca. Complications arise from the beginning when Tom returns from war, bringing with him some captured giants, among them the beautiful Queen Glumdalca. Despite his victory, Huncamunca's mother thwarts Thumb's request for her daughter's hand. She cannot, she says, see one of such low parentage wed to her Huncamunca; her real reason is her own passionate desire for Tom. She is not alone in this: every woman loves him, even the captive Glumdalca. Thumb, however, out-maneuvers them all, steals Huncamunca away from Grizzle, her other suitor, and weds her. Grizzle and Thumb fight; Grizzle dies, and Glumdalca kills herself. Thumb returns again as a victor, only to be swallowed by a cow. The royal house is so upset by the news that everyone stabs everyone else. Surprisingly enough, however, the play ends happily. Merlin appears and with a wave of his wand resurrects all members of the royal household and resuscitates Tom. All merrily sing the final lines of the play that champion restored peace and marital fidelity.

The Opera of Operas offers no coded message for women; it does not present an overt or covert tale that must be interpreted. Instead, it showcases Haywood's versatility and displays her talent for catering to public taste.

Summary

Haywood's four plays represent diverse theatrical expressions. *The Opera of Operas* was the most successful and continues to be well known as one of the best burlesques of the century. *Frederick, Duke of Brunswick-Lunenburgh* is the least successful, filled as it is with orotund speeches and insipid emotions. *The Fair Captive* and *A Wife To be Lett* are the most provoking, as Haywood explores questions pertinent to women that will occupy her for the rest of her writing career, and establishes and initially explores stereotypes that she will continue to examine. *The Fair Captive* especially presents images of female exploitation and enslavement in all their brutality. From the first, Haywood marked off her territory as rebel against such treatment.

Chapter Three
First Novels, 1719–1724

Haywood's triumph in 1719 with her novel *Love in Excess*[1] and her failure with the play *The Fair Captive* decided her future career. After 1721 she began in earnest to explore and exploit the short tale of passion and thwarted love, and soon became, as James Sterling writes, the reigning mistress of the amatory novella, sitting "like Heav'n's bright Minister on High, / Command[ing] the throbbing Breast, and wat'ry Eye."[2] Haywood, of course, did not invent the romance; she was merely shrewd enough to realize its potential as a vehicle offering both a means of escape for her readers and the means for her to entrap them. Caught in rapturous and endless webs of passion and amorous intrigue, escaping to imaginary worlds of seduction and titillation, her readers were unaware of the subtle use she made of the literary form to investigate the pervasive feminine issues of the day. Haywood borrowed the already popular romance mode inherited from France and Spain, and modified it for her own purposes.

The prevailing interest in continental romances and novellas (Italian *novelle* and Spanish *novela exemplare*) was a result of literary tastes fostered by the Restoration. During that time, the English people were both disillusioned and spiritually exhausted; unable to create new literary forms, they produced anglicized versions of the existent continental ones.[3] In the 1650s, for example, the heroic romances of La Calprenède (1614–63) and Madeleine de Scudery (1607–1701) became the models for writers in England. Together with the archetypal French heroic romance *L'Astree,* by D'Urfe, which combined the earlier pastoral and chivalric traditions, these works introduced three important elements into the English fictional scene, as Bridget MacCarthy notes: "authentication of background; the sovereignty of love; and a new conception of the relationship between men and women, whereby women were made the centre of society and the objects of respectful devotion."[4] The constant theme was love, specifically that of a chaste and beautiful lady for a noble and good hero.

Because Calprenède and Scudery offered no insight into or analysis of the inner feelings of their heroes or heroines or even attempted to achieve verisimilitude, by the late 1660s public taste and interest were diverted away from these grandiose romances; instead, short fiction, with its emphasis on psychological acuity, came into fashion. Specifically, it was Cervantes's *Exemplary Novels,* translated by Mappe (1640; reprinted in England 1694, 1708, and 1728), that introduced a more believable, realistic element into current fiction. These Spanish tales concentrated on the struggle of lovers to be united or, even more plausibly, depicted the efforts of an abandoned girl to catch her elusive lover. Concurrently, the Italian novella with its central theme of sensual love and eroticism also became popular.[5] It quickly challenged the place of the heroic romance because of the public's demand for realism, and the growing interest in the comedy of manners also supported this vogue. Hack writers of the period introduced works overflowing with passionate love, high-flown sentimentality, and exaggerated emotions. Persecuted virtue, abduction, and attempted rapes became the stock devices to move the reader from bathos to ecstacy and to underscore the eternal contest of good and evil. Haywood turned these forms to her own advantage and examined the position of women by manipulating these patterns.

Love in Excess

Haywood entered this literary milieu in 1719 and stunned the reading public with *Love in Excess; or, The Fatal Enquiry,*[6] a tale, as Whicher writes, of "the *vie amoroureuse* of Count D'Elmont, a hero with none of the wit, but with all the gallantry of the rakes of late Restoration comedy. Two parts of the novel relate the aristocratic intrigues of D'Elmont and his friends; the third shows him . . . reform'd and a model of constancy."[7] The work reflects Haywood's theatre experience, as its three parts function as acts, with the whole "play" concluding in stereotypical fashion with the marriages of all couples. Scenes are played until every possible emotion has been wrung from them, and the characters tend to be reminiscent of William Congreve's ever-popular Mirabell and Millamant, or George Etherege's Sir Fopling Flutter. As Whicher notes, the novel at this early date was merely "a looser and more extended series of sensational adventures"[8] patterned on the act structure of Restoration drama.

The main plot of *Love in Excess,* although excessively long, is perhaps one of Haywood's easiest to follow. Count D'Elmont returns from the French wars and becomes the toast of the town. Celebrated and lionized by both sexes, he is sought after especially by the scheming Alovisa. Unfortunately, he is busy intriguing with Amena, the first of several ingenues with whom he is infatuated, and has no time for Alovisa's charms and demands. Full of wrath and jealousy, Alovisa plots the end of Amena and D'Elmont's love affair. On the evening of their assignation in the Tuilleries she sets fire to Amena's house, and the lovers return to find their absence noted, Amena's house smoldering, and their return to her garden blocked. In desperation, Amena seeks shelter with Alovisa. But Alovisa's treachery and her perfidious love for D'Elmont are soon revealed, and Amena, totally undone, exclaims "who wou'd . . . wish to stay in a World so full of Falshood'" (1, p. 53), and willingly retreats to St. Dennis's monastery. Faced with Amena's departure, D'Elmont succumbs to his ambitious desires and marries the malicious Alovisa, who has promised to help fulfill all his wishes.

The match is a failure from the beginning. D'Elmont and Alovisa soon quarrel, and he consoles himself by falling in love with his ward, the "matchless Melliora" (1, p. 59). "The Count's secret Passion for Melliora grew stronger by his endeavoring to suppress it . . . [and] he grew almost distracted with the continual restraint he was forc'd to put on all his Words and Actions" (1, p. 88). His restraint is minimal, however, and page after page recounts his unsuccessful attempts to seduce and rape the girl. With each assault he becomes more bold, Melliora is more frightened, and Alovisa grows more enraged. In an attempt to take revenge upon her husband, Alovisa plots his downfall with her lover, the Baron D'Espernay, but through miscalculations and ill timing, both the Baron and Alovisa are killed by D'Elmont in a rather bloody struggle. Nor does Melliora escape unscathed, for she had fallen in love with D'Elmont but could openly admit her feelings only to herself. Her passionate self cried out to be taken and mastered by him, while her rational side proclaimed his extreme unsuitableness. Melliora "felt Torments unconceivable, yet the strength of her virtue enabled her to keep it, and she return[ed] to the Monastery, where she had been educated, carrying with her nothing of that Peace of Mind with which she left it" (3, p. 170).

In an effort to forget the "matchless Melliora," D'Elmont travels on the continent. Although attraction is great, and numerous women run away, poison themselves, or die for love of him (one, in fact, even disguises herself as Fidelio, a footpage, and serves D'Elmont in this menial way), the man is unaware of the havoc he wreaks. In an effort to try and forget Melliora, D'Elmont helps her brother pursue his own romance (the mirroring or double plot is a standard Haywood technique), and while doing so again encounters Melliora, who has been abducted from the convent and is pursued by the Marquis de Sanguillier. In a thrilling finish, Melliora deserts the Marquis at the very moment of the exchange of their marriage vows and runs to D'Elmont. The Marquis, ever undaunted, quickly turns his affection to an old flame, while D'Elmont and Melliora marry. The happy ending is marred only by Fidelio's self-revelation and death; otherwise, *Love in Excess* concludes with three marriages and six lives supposedly lived out in conjugal bliss.

Because of the length of this first novel (she did not write another in three volumes until *The History of Miss Betsy Thoughtless*), the characters are drawn in more depth than is usual for Haywood, yet, in essence, they remain the stereotypes she was to use again and again. The three rakes, Baron D'Espernay, D'Elmont, and his brother Brillian, value women as sexual playthings; the Baron's view— "Women are taught by custom, to deny what most they covet, and to seem angry when they are best pleas'd[;] believe me, D'Elmont, that the most rigid Virtue of 'em all, never yet hated a Man for those faults which Love occasions" (2, pp. 99–100)—is shared by all. *Love in Excess* tells of the rakes' reformation, however; at the end, the Baron is dead and D'Elmont and Brillian have learned their lesson.

The women characters are more important, however. Haywood uses a mirror or double-inversion technique with minor characters, echoing the adventures of the major figures and thus emphasizing the rape/virtue-in-distress theme that highlights her constant topic of feminine exploitation. She also employs a technique of antithetical pairing of her female characters. For example, the passive, ultra-submissive Amena is contrasted with the aggressive, manipulative, almost Machiavellian Alovisa. Amena personifies the woman whose easy capitulation to the male makes her of prime importance in tales exploiting female weakness and dependence. Alovisa, on the other hand, represents the often repressed side of femininity, that side of aggression and passion that Haywood endeavors to unmask in an effort to create a healthy woman. Alovisa is similarly contrasted with Melliora; when faced with noncompliance with her will, Alovisa "rav'd, she tore her hair and Face, and in the Extremity of her Anguish was ready to lay violent hands on her own Life" (1, p. 8), while Melliora, when faced with her father's death, sat "in a fix'd and silent sorrow, (tho' inwardly toss'd with various violent agitations)" (1, p. 63). Melliora, the matchless beauty, is the first in a long line of persecuted maidens who manage to remain undefiled and marry only for true love at the conclusion of their adventures. Melliora and Alovisa become Haywood's critique of women in the eighteenth century and represent her first attempt to deal with the woman question in her fiction. Melliora is a clear paradigm of the women who occupy the false position that men create for them in the real world; Alovisa is Haywood's comment on this female and her position; although she is not an ideal, she is important as a manifestation of Haywood's anger at the treatment of women. In her later romances, Haywood frequently contrasted the submissive, docile heroine with a diabolic female who was actually her own aggressive self in disguise. In each case, she covertly expressed her own anger at the scene that she witnessed.

In the end, Haywood uses this romance form as a way to investigate and perhaps challenge the accepted doctrines of reason that governed the age. That is, in the final triumph of virtue over vice, reason over feeling, and order over the chaos created by the passions, Haywood bows to the convention that depicts masculine superiority saving assaulted feminine sensibility. Yet it is an uneasy victory at best, for Haywood's novels, even these of her early years, at least question the masculine rules of society. Alovisa exists to express Haywood's anger and to question male supremacy; in subsequent works, other extraordinarily aggressive women are all equally viable as subtle symbols of this rage.

Haywood was very careful to couch her revolutionary questionings and tactics in a palatable form. Quick to recognize the tastes of the reading public, she based the majority of her novels and romances, those of both these early years and her later period, on the myth of persecuted virtue. This concept, which sees the female as innocent, virtuous, extraordinarily sensitive, and victimized by the social order created by male interests, was ideal to her rebellious position. R. F. Brissenden observes that the "emergence of the theme of

virtue in distress in the widest sense grew out of an awareness of
the distance which separated moral idealism and the world of practical action."[9] The theme becomes a simplification of the focus found
in society. Unable openly to challenge existing rules that were
established by the male, Haywood challenged her readers' awareness
and forced them to become cognizant of their situation through her
manipulation of their favorite romance pattern.

Eighteenth-century women novelists used the romance form, Patricia Meyer Spacks observes, to "communicate the world's im-
pingements on the personal, while expressing also the fantasies
through which women combat impingement."[10] She continues,
"Through the conventions of romance women tell themselves and
one another the meaning of their fate."[11] For the less astute, Haywood's tales provide adventure and escape; for the more aware, her
stories challenge existing beliefs and customs and sow the seeds of
revolutionary change in society.

The British Recluse

The surprising success of *Love in Excess* (five editions before the
collected edition of 1724) convinced Haywood that she had at last
found a way to support herself. Unwilling to be victimized by the
male society, she prepared to do battle with sexual and societal
inequality. Her heroines often did the same. A great many women,
Haywood observed, were not ready to sacrifice themselves and pine
away in obscurity waiting for male recognition. A new breed of
independent, self-sufficient women was forming at that time, and
Eliza Haywood was a leader of this quiet rebellion. Far from ac-
cepting acquiescent attitudes and slavelike drudgery, Haywood's
characters, like their creator, went out of their way to prove their
independence. Her second novel is the story of two such new women.

The British Recluse; or, The Secret History of Cleomira, Suppos'd Dead
(1722),[12] is about Cleomira and Belinda, who share the dubious
honor of having been seduced by the handsome Lysander. Their
stories are complementary halves to the same, sad tale of persecuted
virtue.

Cleomira's tale is easily told. "Bred up in all the Pomp and Pride
of Quality" (1, p. 16), she is unused to the unfair ways of the world.
After her father's death, she and her mother move to the country,
but the "sudden change from all the Liberties of the World to the

most strict Confinement" (p. 17) is absolute "death" to Cleomira. Languishing and bored, she finally obtains permission to return to the court for a ball. There she meets and falls instantly in love with Lysander—"His Air! his Shape! his Face! were more than human! [and I] . . . was plung'd in a wild sea of Passion, before I had Time to *know*, or stem the Danger" (p. 19). "So blinded with . . . Passion" (p. 27), Cleomira runs away with this godlike man so that they can indulge their illicit passion. Cleomira becomes a sex object.

Once in London, Lysander's ardor quickly and predictably cools; Cleomira is torn with jealousy when she sees the man with his latest conquest. She threatens to kill herself, but does not take enough poison and only causes herself discomfort. When she regains consciousness and learns how calmly Lysander has faced her imminent demise, she is confronted with the truth of her situation. *"Reason, unobscured by Passion,* shew'd me how truly wretched I had made myself " (p. 44), she tells us. *"Reason,* at last, has gain'd a Conquest over all that softness which has hitherto betrayed me to contempt.— Now I will live and *Love* alone shall die" (p. 77). Fortunately, her native reason reasserts itself, and she decides to retire from the sinful London scene.

Belinda, too, is overcome by the handsome Lysander, and she discards a heroic suitor (predictably enough, named Mr. Worthy) in favor of this infamous rake. More fortunate than Cleomira, she is saved by Worthy just before Lysander can realize his base desires. Unfortunately, Worthy is wounded in the rescue attempt, but recovers only to wed Belinda's sister. Faced with such a calamity, Belinda, like Cleomira, chooses a solitary life away from the world of Lysander and his kind.

These two characters are Haywood's first full-length portraits of the new, independent woman whom she was so anxious to promote and champion. They prove to be survivors; although undone by the exploiting male, they do not allow themselves to be destroyed by him; although initially victimized, they do not remain so. There is no need for disguised authorial anger as found in *Love in Excess*'s Alovisa, Melantha, or Ciamara; Haywood openly declares her detestation of the male's treatment of women.

The British Recluse is an important book for Haywood to have written so early in her career, as in it she reveals her intention to attack the male community. At a time when one would expect her to court the public's favor, it is worth noting that she felt sure

enough of her own powers and abilities as a novelist to assert without
reserve what she felt was important: female independence from and
survival without the male.

The Injur'd Husband

In an apparent effort to cater to popular taste, Haywood returns
in her next novel to the more usual depiction of a society of dominant
males and chastened women. With its presentation of the "Worst
of Women" (p. 117) in the person of the Baroness de Tortilleé, *The
Injur'd Husband*[13] becomes almost a satire of *The British Recluse*.
Independence, self-sufficiency, and control become arrogance, greed,
and fanaticism as portrayed by the cruel and lascivious antics of the
Baroness.

The Baroness de Tortilleé is a wicked woman. Determined to
satisfy her insatiable lusts, she marries the foolish, doting and wealthy
Baron:

> If this woman had been possess'd of the smallest Grain of Honour, Grat-
> itude, or even common Good-Nature, she wou'd have endeavour'd by her
> future Manner of Behaviour, to retrieve the Errors of the past. . . . But
> she was wholly dead to such Considerations: She look'd on the large Fortune
> she was now become Mistress of, only as a larger Means to gratify her
> Inclinations. . . . She had no Sense of Honour. (pp. 127–28)

The Baroness continues her premarital lifestyle—prostitution—and
gives "a loose to all the Sallies of her ungovernable Passions, imagining her Quality a sufficient Sanction for her Vices" (p. 128). She
even retains her pimp, DuLache. Her husband, fool that he is, is
completely taken in; "so much was he deluded by her Artifices,
that even her Vices appeared Virtues" (p. 128), and Haywood concludes, "no Woman that ever liv'd was Mistress of more Artifice,
nor had less the Appearance of being so" (p. 129).

After enjoying several affairs with men DuLache procures for her,
the Baroness covets the handsome Beauclair, the romantic hero of
the novel, who is in love with Montamour. In spite of his devotion
to another, the Baroness manages temporarily to capture Beauclair's
affections and blacken his reputation, and drug the Baron and send
him to the country so that she can carry on her intrigues with
Beauclair and others. Her plans miscarry, however. Cured of his
false illness, the Baron returns and attacks DuLache and Beauclair,
who he believes is in league against him; during the fight the Baron

is stabbed by DuLache. One "Vrayment," a witness to the fight, turns out to be Montamour in disguise. She testifies to save Beauclair's life, and they manage to survive because "she had that Constancy of Mind, and steadiness of Resolution, which . . . other[s] *boast,* but rarely *prove* themselves Masters of" (p. 170). Montamour is governed by generosity, not revenge, and fortunately, Beauclair perceives the goodness of her character in time. DuLache and the other guilty men are broken on the wheel; the Baroness takes poison and dies; Beauclair and Montamour are married. Good and bad are rewarded in true romance fashion.

In spite of its romantic happy ending, *The Injur'd Husband* reveals Haywood's interior anger. Couched behind the romantic story for her readers to uncover should they discard their conservative bias is the true story about men, that is, there are no good ones: they are weak—the Baron; cunning—DuLache; and villainous—Toncarr and Lesonge. Even the supposed hero comes in for a lot of criticism. He is "Impatience [*sic.*] of Indignities" (p. 141) to his character and far too gullible. The fact that he believes the rumors created by the Baroness about his beloved does not speak well of his character. Since men do not have a strong leading role, the plot is engineered by the Baroness herself. Like Alovisa, Cleomira, and Belinda, she is aggressive, even demonic, and she expresses Haywood's feelings about women taking charge of their own lives. Although submission is depicted with Montamour's marriage to Beauclair, it is a side issue to Haywood's major presentation in which she opposes the strong, vigorous woman against the subtle, submissive one in an attempt to exaggerate the extremes of female behavior. Since her readers would unconsciously identify with Montamour, Haywood underscores their plight by telling a tale of the girl's exploitation and harassment.

Idalia

Haywood's next novel, *Idalia; or, The Unfortunate Mistress* (1723),[14] can be ranked among her finest works. Unlike the case in so many of her literary effusions, she portrays characters in some depth while probing the psychological basis for their actions. Idalia's world is not the unwavering black-and-white one portrayed so often in fiction, and the reader is able to experience the heroine's romantic dilemmas and learn from them while Haywood provides an interior view of her mind.

It is the story of the Venetian beauty, Idalia, whose love interests take her throughout most of Italy. [15] She is so beautiful that "Imagination cannot form a Face more exquisitely lovely; such Majesty, such Sweetness, such a Regularity in all her Features, accompany'd with an Air at once so soft, so striking, that while she *commanded* she *allur'd,* and *forc'd* what she *entreated*" (p. 2). Idalia, however, is ruled by vanity, and she is held up, not as a positive model, but as an example of what not to become. One cannot totally blame Idalia for her conduct and her eventual fate. As Haywood writes, "The Greatness of her Spirit (which from her Childhood had been untameable, or was render'd so thro too great Indulgence of her doating Parents) made her unable to endure controll, disdainful of advice, obstinate, and peremptory in following her own *Will* to what Extremes soever it led her" (pp. 2–3).

It is just this lack of focus and of education that causes all her problems. Because of her great beauty, she is pursued by numerous suitors; one, Florez, is more insistent than the others. When her father forbids future contact between the two, she is piqued, "not that she was really in *love* with him, or had yet any notion of that Passion; but *Vanity,* the reigning Faculty of her Soul, prompted her to use her utmost efforts for the retrieving a Heart she began to fear was estranged" (p. 4). Idalia disregards her father's commands and resolves to do what she desires. In the meantime, despicable Florez is ready to bring about her ruin and arranges an assignation, at which time his patron, Don Ferdinand, who has gone in his place, rapes Idalia. (The ubiquity of evil is a constant theme.)

Rape scenes like the following always show Haywood at her best: "What was now the Distraction of this unhappy Lady, waked from her Dream of Vanity to certain Ruin! unavoidable Destruction! She rav'd, she tore, did all that Woman could; but all in vain!—In the Midst of Shrieks and Tremblings, Cries, Curses, Swoonings, the impatient Ferdinand perpetrated his Intent, and finish'd her Undoing" (p. 17). The reader is made to feel sorry for Idalia; she has been victimized; the action is all on the part of the male. In other such passages, however, although the rape is forced by the man, there is a slight unconscious desire on the woman's part. Haywood wrote a third type of rape scene in which the woman is the aggressor (e.g., in *Love in Excess* Ciamara intends to rape D'Elmont), and the language is loaded in an effort to titillate the readers. In all three kinds of rape, innocence is betrayed; Haywood manipulates the scenes, shifting the focus depending upon who is innocent.

In *Idalia* there is no question of who is betrayed. Florez and Don Ferdinand abandon her to Henriquez and rush off in an attempt to save their own lives. Henriquez is charmed by Idalia and is soon in love with her. He and Florez fight over her and both are killed. When Henriquez's brother, Myrtano, brings Idalia word of the duel and its outcome, he, too, falls passionately in love with her. She, strangely enough, remains placid: "there was a happy Instability in this Lady's Nature, which prevented her from regretting any Thing for a long Time together" (pp. 35–36). This instability fails her when she meets Myrtano, and she suddenly learns what it is to love and be in love. On the very brink of yet another seduction/rape, however, Idalia's will asserts itself and she decamps for a monastery in Verona, proclaiming, "I still am Mistress of my self,—my own unconquerable Will!" (p. 64).

But peace eludes her even on holy ground, and soon, disguised as a country lass (in an attempt to recover lost innocence), Idalia decides to go in search of Myrtano. En route to Naples, she falls victim to the evil schemes of a ship's captain, but is saved when the ship is captured by Barbary corsairs; then she is caught in a shipwreck and is cast on shore only to be rescued by some hospitable cottagers. Disguised as a man, she continues her journey until, finally arriving in Rome, she finds Myrtano, who has married Donna Antonia. Unfortunately, Idalia makes a very handsome man, and soon Antonia falls in love with her. When Idalia's sex is revealed, Antonia flies into a jealous rage, tries to kill both Idalia and her husband with her sword, and gains her revenge by forcing the Pope, who had come to pass judgment on the case, to separate the two lovers.

In the meantime, Idalia is forcibly separated from Myrtano again; and, treated like a courtesan, she is pursued by all the gallants. Still in Rome, she sees Florez, to whom she attributes all her misfortunes. She determines to kill him, but stabs Myrtano, who has come in his place, by mistake. Overcome by his death, Idalia stabs herself.

Idalia; or, the Unfortunate Mistress is plainly melodramatic, but the perils of the heroine hold the reader's attention. Just when one thinks that all that can happen has, Idalia is captured again and virtue is persecuted once more. Here, however, this theme is given a new twist; rather than good ultimately triumphing with Idalia's

rescue by the hero, Haywood offers a rather jaundiced view of besieged virtue trying to survive in a world of villains. Forced to
become a "wretched Wanderer thro' the pitiless World" (p. 27),
Idalia typifies this theme of innocence betrayed. Virtue dies with
her, as do order and justice. At the time of her death, Florez is
unapprehended, and what Haywood calls "the Justice of Heaven"
(p. 162) has yet to occur. The world view presented here, like that
of Swift's *Gulliver's Travels* and Hogarth's *The Rake's Progress,* is dark
indeed. Chaos has come again and has been visited on the innocent
female. *Idalia* is not like much of the other popular literature. It
offers no fairy-tale magic for the majority of women. Haywood again
uses the melodrama first to enmesh her readers and then underline
women's persecuted state.

The novel is also important because it reflects a new ability of
Haywood to integrate setting and character. For example, the open-
ing of the second book with its description of the forest underscores
Idalia's own emotional and psychological entanglement, while the
storm and shipwreck propel her to her own inner destruction. Haywood will continue this probing of the feminine psyche in the
majority of her novels. The integration of mood and setting, perhaps
naively and superficially achieved here, reaches its climax in *Philidore
and Placentia* (1727).

Lasselia

Lasselia; or the Self-Abandon'd[16] is another story of female exploitation, although it does not end with the heroine's death like *Idalia,*
but only with her incarceration in a convent. It is tinged with
bitterness, authorial anger, and frustration.

The story begins in the court of Louis XIV. Lasselia, the beautiful,
placid heroine, suddenly attracts the eye of the lascivious King, and
"as artless as she was, and as indifferent an Opinion as she had
of Love, she easily perceiv'd she had inspir'd him with that Desire . . . and was so far from being proud of her Power, that it gave
her a very great Uneasiness" (p. 11). Upholding her virtue and
disdaining to become one of the King's mistresses, Lasselia leaves
the court and retires to the country. She does not find shelter and
sanctuary, however. Meeting Monsieur De L'Amye, she is so overwhelmed by his "Form so perfectly compleat" (p. 19) that she soon
casts reason aside and rushes headlong into an affair. Fortunately

for Lasselia, her lover, whatever else he may be, is honest: "he never *promis'd* more than he *performed*—his *Professions* never outsoar'd his Meaning" (p. 43). Their interlude is of short duration, for the "Hand of Fate . . . dashes the short-liv'd Bliss" (p. 45). One of De L'Amye's disgruntled former mistresses, Douxmouries, discovers the pair and informs his wife of the amour. In the denouement, the conventional status quo is maintained; Lasselia is "persuaded" to enter a nunnery, where she becomes a model of piety, and the De L'Amyes are reconciled.

Once more, Haywood has told of female exploitation. Had Lasselia not been sexually harassed by the King, she would not have met De L'Amye and fallen in love with him. Like the heroines of the other early novels, Lasselia is used and discarded by the male, thus becoming a symbolic representation of eighteenth-century women. Haywood speaks out against the injustice of the system that allows for such behavior and condemns the male population that is its perpetrator.

The Rash Resolve

The last novel of this early period, *The Rash Resolve; or, The Untimely Discovery* (1723),[17] offers another troublesome picture of the annihilation of female consciousness by male manipulation. It is the story of Emanuella, who is first robbed and then brutally imprisoned by her guardian, Don Pedro; she is rescued by his compassionate son, Don Marco, and then goes on to Madrid, where she meets and falls in love with Emilius. Emanuella, like Idalia and Lasselia, abrogates her reason and follows her passion instead; she succumbs to male rule and dominance, and willingly follows Emilius in all things.

Initially very naive, "entirely free from all Deceit and Artifice Herself" (p. 3), Emanuella creates idealistic fantasies and expects life to be like them. Like the majority of Haywood's heroines, she is unable to distinguish appearance from reality and continues to work for the realizations of her dreams. When she meets Emilius, for example, "a Person to her sight so conformable to the *Idea* she had created in her Mind, of what would please her . . . she could not presently distinguish whether it was still the same delightful Vision her extensive Fancy had dress'd up with all the Ornaments of Art and Nature, or a real Substance" (p. 40). She casts an aura

of the heroic over Emilius, "and was by this time too far enter'd
into the Fatal Maze, to be able to extricate herself" (p. 47). But
like the majority of Haywood's men, Emilius is a wolf in fancy
dress. He soon abandons Emanuella because of the scurrilous lies
told him by Berilla, the antagonistic, aggressive, demonic parody
of Emanuella. Berilla, "more than Barbarian" (p. 60), engineers not
only Emilius's abandonment of Emanuella, but the heroine's retreat
to a convent.

Emanuella runs away having learned, she thinks, of the perfi-
diousness of man; "in knowing one, I know the whole deceiving
Sex—Nor will I be a second time betray'd" (p. 65). For a time,
she regains her equilibrium; however, she is not allowed to remain
in the convent, where she might possibly also have regained some
of her lost selfhood. Instead, she must leave after the birth of Vic-
torinus, her son by Emilius. Emanuella undertakes a search for her
lover, and after several other twists and turns of the plot, is reunited
with him. Emilius's wife magnanimously resigns her claim when
she hears Emanuella's tale, thereby counteracting all the perfidious-
ness of Berilla. At last, knowing that there are indeed some "good
women," Emanuella dies.

The Rash Resolve continues to investigate the question of women's
place and their role. Women continue to be exploited, but it is
noteworthy that Haywood's anger has increased to such proportions
that she has women destroying other women: there is no sanctuary
for the female. She must constantly be on her guard if she is to
maintain her selfhood.

Secret Histories, Novels, and Poems

Between 1719 and 1724 Haywood established herself as the arbitress of the passionately throbbing breast and watery eye. Clearly,
with her first six novels, she had become the foremost writer of the
titillating pop-fiction of her day. From middle-class ladies of leisure
to the serving maids in the kitchen, these romances were read in
nearly every household. The first period of Haywood's career was
brought to a close with the publication in 1725 of her four-volume
Secret Histories, Novels, and Poems (already partially issued in 1724);
the set was reissued in 1732 and 1742. Additional stories were
collected and issued in a new edition that was published in 1727
in two volumes.

The popularity of *Secret Histories* led Haywood to include some samples of her verse in the final volume of the first edition. Derivative at best, they record in rather hackneyed and affected terms the sufferings and tribulations of both the lover and the beloved. The speaker in the untitled poem beginning, "Weary, detesting all Society" succinctly describes the typical state of Haywood's lovers:

> my divided Soul
> Yields now to *this,* and then to *that* Controul;
> And whilst I neither dispossest,
> Both with convulsive Fury rend my bleeding Breast.
> (p. 278, ll. 36–39)

The usual Petrarchian love conventions are used to excess, and the reader is left with shallow, hackneyed expressions and poorly constructed verse.

The final assessment of Haywood's early novels cannot be so facile. True, they gave the eighteenth-century reading public the usual romance conventions, techniques, and rhetoric, but more important, they introduced the themes, characters, and situations that Haywood continued to explore and develop throughout her career. The theme of persecuted virtue is well established, together with questions regarding traditional roles and positions imposed by the male society on the female. For example, *Love in Excess* offers straightforward portraits of the unrepentant rake, reformed rake, and persecuted maiden; *The British Recluse, The Injur'd Husband, Idalia, Lasselia,* and *The Rash Resolve* introduce nontraditional female roles or solutions and ultimately present a challenge to conventionally ordered society.

Chapter Four

Duncan Campbell Pamphlets, 1720–1725

Haywood's popularity from 1719 to 1724 was founded upon her ability to portray the throbbing breast and panting heart better than any of her contemporaries. Her own interests, however, included more than weeping heroines and boisterous heroes. Collaborating with Daniel Defoe on the Duncan Campbell pamphlets between 1720 and 1725 allowed Haywood to indulge her taste in the sensational.

Campbell's fame as a deaf-mute prophet had been established earlier through articles in *The Tatler* (no. 14) and *The Spectator* (nos. 323, 474, and 560). By 1720, however, public interest had begun to wane, until Defoe, with a minimum amount of collaboration from Haywood, wrote *The History of the Life and Adventures of Mr. Duncan Campbell.*[1] Defoe's hand is obvious, as he writes in the persona of Campbell in the Epistle Dedicatory:

Instead of making [the tale of my life] a Bill of Fare out of patchwork Romances of polluting Scandal; the good old [Defoe] who wrote the Adventures of my Life, has made it his Business to treat them with a great variety of entertaining Passages, which always terminate in morals that tend to the edification of all Readers. (p. iv)

The book is largely devoted to discussions of the perception of genii, of spirits, magic, and second sight. (Some sixteen years later Haywood would use some of this magical lore in her portrait of the evil magician, Ochihatou, in *The Adventures of Eovaai*.)

Early chapters tracing Campbell's birth, travels, and exploits soon give way to "The Method of teaching Deaf and Dumb Persons to write, read, and understand a Language" (Chapter 3), "A Philosophical Discourse Concerning the Second Sight" (Chapter 7), and "A Dissertation upon Magick under all its branches" (Chapter 8). There are few hints of passion within the pages of this ponderous volume. As the Epistle Dedicatory states, "Instead of seducing young, innocent, unwary Minds into the vicious Delight, which is too often taken in reading the gay and bewitching Chimeras of the Cabalists . . . my ancient Friend, the writer, strikes at the very Root of these Superstitions, and shews them, how they may be satisfy'd in their several Curiosities, by having recourse to Me" (p. v). Thus the blooming beauty, the seamstress, the housekeeper, and the chambermaid ask love advice, and Campbell's counsel is written in a highly realistic vein quite unlike Haywood's usual mode. Whicher suggests that the few amorous details found in the work were contributed by William Bond,[2] a mutual acquaintance of both Defoe and Haywood, and it is most probable that it was through this friendship that Haywood got involved with the project.

The next in the series, *A Spy upon the Conjuror; or, A Collection of Surprising Stories* (1724),[3] is known to be entirely Haywood's work. All the letters and inquiries are concerned with love, and the stories relate to love affairs in which one of the parties invokes Campbell's assistance.[4] Gone is the realistic advice proffered by Defoe in the earlier volume; in its place we find Haywood's usual romantic leanings. The chapter headings are enough to illustrate this: "A Strange story of a young lady, who came to ask the name of her husband" (Chapter 5), "A Whimsical Story of an Old Lady who wanted a Husband" (Chapter 6), and "A Story of my Lady Love-Puppy" (Chapter 9). Love and passion are the mainstay of this second volume of the Duncan Campbell collection, and the author is quick to give exciting advice.

All, however, is not titillation. Although Haywood does not seem greatly interested in the covert tales, she does manage to exhibit a little of the woman's story. She portrays the total control men exert over women using Duncan Campbell's ability to see the past and future of unknown persons. When he is solicited by women for advice about their love affairs, Haywood demonstrates his control over them as he reveals their innermost secrets. A "fine woman, of middle Age, and two Daughters" (p. 58) have come to inquire about the daughters' husbands. Instead of revealing their future, Campbell exposes their mother's past by revealing that one daughter is illegitimate. The mother is so impressed with Campbell's perspicacity that she becomes one of his most ardent admirers; she literally enslaves herself to him. Such acts are repeated again and again. *A Spy upon the Conjuror* desexes women; Campbell's discernment does not allow them any freedom; they are not permitted to harbor secret thoughts; they are exposed, anatomized under his gaze.

Apparently, the popular temperament was stimulated by these two volumes, for in 1725 a forty-page pamphlet entitled *The Dumb Projector: Being a Surprizing Account of a Trip to Holland made by Mr. Duncan Campbell*[5] was issued. Haywood's story, although ostensibly concerned with Campbell's land and sea adventures, gives greater emphasis to his amatory conquests. But Haywood approaches these with no zest, and the volume, in general, is disappointing.

The last pamphlet was published in 1725 under the title *The Friendly Daemon; or, The Generous Apparition* and was reprinted in 1732 as *The Secret Memoirs of the Late Mr. Duncan Campbell*.[6] Internal evidence suggests that the work is a product of both Defoe's and Haywood's labor. Chapters "On Witchcraft" (Chapter 4), "On Predestination" (Chapter 7), and "On Apparition" (Chapter 10) are found together with letters "From a Lady, who, from the Depth of Misery, was suddenly raised to Happiness" (Chapter 3), "From a young Lady very much in Love" (Chapter 8), and "From a new-married Lady" (Chapter 12). Mrs. Haywood was the only one to use the form of letters supposedly addressed to the prophet, and those in the *Secret Memoirs* are similar enough to ones in *A Spy upon the Conjuror* to ensure her authorship.

The Duncan Campbell pamphlets were popular, and the Haywood-Defoe collaboration proved to be profitable for both writers. It is interesting to note, as Whicher does, that

Eliza Haywood, in a contemporary opinion, out ranked Defoe almost as far as an interpreter of the heart as he surpassed her in concocting an account of a new marvel or a tale of strange adventure. The arbitress of the passions indeed wrote nothing to compare in popularity with "Robinson Crusoe," but before 1740 her "Love in Excess" ran through as many editions as "Moll Flanders" and its abridgments, while "Idalia; or, the Unfortunate Mistress" had been reprinted three times separately and twice with her collected novels before a reissue of Defoe's "Fortunate Mistress" was undertaken.[7]

The Duncan Campbell pamphlets reenforced Haywood's claim to be chief "Arbitress of Passion"[8] and firmly established her ability to compete with the recognized literary figures of her day. Her work with Defoe also clearly exhibited the two strains that the English novel would follow in later years: the picaresque tradition, taken up by Defoe, and the sentimental novel—the novel of the heart—established by Haywood.

Chapter Five
Haywood as Translator

Haywood's initial success as a writer of romances cannot be doubted. Her collaboration with Defoe and the numerous editions of *Love in Excess, Idalia,* and *The Rash Resolve* together with her collected works of 1724 and 1727 are proof of her popularity. In these early novels, Haywood was following her native genius, to be sure, but she was not unfamiliar with the works of her continental predecessors. From 1721 with her "paraphrase" of the ever-popular *Portuguese Letters (Letters from a Lady of Quality to a Chevalier)* to her 1742 translation of de Mouhy's *The Virtuous Villager; or, Virgin's Victory,* Haywood's career was interlaced with her translating efforts. In all, she translated eight popular continental romances for her English audience, and it was this work that helped her learn her craft. For example, she found romance situations and characters, image patterns and motifs, themes of persecuted innocence and virtue in distress, together with the cult of the heroic romance and its exaggerated emphasis on love and gallantry that became the basis for her own sentimental novels.

Continental love stories not only provided her with stock characters and situations, but the popular works of Madames de Lafayette and de Villedieu introduced her to a new writing technique. Unlike the highly bombastic heroic romances, these works attempted a more realistic assessment of the love situation and offered psychological penetration unequaled in the French romance form. The major emphasis in each is on the heroine, on the psychological disorders that love produces within her, and on her own attempts to overcome this inordinate passion. It was this pattern that became the hallmark of Haywood's own novels.

Letters from a Lady of Quality

Haywood's first translation, *Letters from a Lady of Quality to a Chevalier* (1721),[1] was of the *Lettre nouvelles de Monsieur Boursault . . . avec frieze lettres amoureuses d'une dame à un cavalier.* (She herself considered the work a "paraphrase," indicating, I believe, the liberties she took with the actual text.) The collected letters do not tell a linear story, but chronicle the subplot of the fears, doubts, jealousies, disappointments, sufferings, and ecstasies of a married woman for her French lover, who, by the final letter, has abandoned her and returned to France. Her plight—how she "may love, and yet be innocent" (p. 3)—is prototypical for the eighteenth-century woman and the novella becomes a recital of virtue's trial. On the one hand, the lady declares, "I have already told you, and I shall continue to tell you, that I consent to have the highest Esteem, the most tender Regard, and the sincerest Friendship imaginable for you; but nothing further" (p. 10); on the other hand, she agrees to meet her lover secretly in the Tuilleries and continue the correspondence if "you follow my Directions, and mak[e] the superscription to another, deceive even the very Person from whose hands I take [the letters]" (p. 15). Her recital displays a constant battle between passion and reason, of "Agitations [and] . . . inexpressible Inquietudes which torture" (p. 23) her. She writes, "my Reason, my Prudence, my Honour, my Duty are *against*, but are not forcible enough to *prevent* the liberty I take in favour of my Passion" (p. 29), and continues her "affair" with the chevalier.

The *Letters* are strangely moving. The speaker, for example, astutely assesses her lover's movements into her heart: "You have found the way to wind yourself into my very Soul, robb'd me of all the Means of Opposition, and, by an artful yielding, conquer!—You are become so much a part of me, that, methinks, I should have no Reserve, no separate Views" (p. 60). The book thus perceptively underscores the total possession that occurs in a woman in love. She is left nothing, not even her own mind. The protagonist writes from her soul of the agony and ecstasy of this kind of total self-abandonment and of the resultant battle between her reason and duty and her passion.[2]

In this early work, Haywood begins to investigate the plight of women by displaying the double influence to which they are subject. The *Letters* actually exhibit the rhetorical technique of palimpsestic, double writing that became the basis of her style. The surface story is one of abandonment and misplaced love; the hidden tale is one of anger and hate. What Haywood finds is that writing can reveal what otherwise is often too painful to express: "Paper cannot blush, and our Thoughts, in spite of us, will often take a greater liberty in expressing themselves that way, than the natural Bashfulness of Virtue will permit 'em to do any other" (p. 6). Her works waken her readers from the "Deluding Dream" (p. 7) of the principal story and reveal what is at the heart of woman and at the core of her writings. Although she gives public voice to women's duty, her actions belie her words, and her subtextual meaning is one of rebellion. *Letters from a Lady of Quality* is Haywood's own testament to the female condition.

La Belle Assemblée

Madame de Gomez's *La Belle Assemblée; or, The Adventures of Six Days,*[3] translated by Haywood in 1724, is another seminal work in her development as a novelist. Modeled on Boccaccio's *novelle, La Belle Assemblée* relates tales of passion interlarded with long conversations on love, morals, politics, and wit; the whole is presented in the framework of a six-day visit to the country by sophisticated court people. Again, "love in excess" is the theme and the vignettes tell of "Nature outdone by Love," "The Triumph of Virtue," "Love Victorious over Death," and "Heroick Love." Part 1 (1724) contains eighteen stories in four volumes; the second part, *L'Entretien des Beaux Esprits* (1734),[4] was greatly reduced in scope and contains only fourteen stories crowded into two volumes; its focus on plot, with a paucity of character development and a lack of other intention but that of telling a story, make it an exceedingly dull work, and certainly not one that offered Haywood any sort of narrative challenge. In general, there is a sort of sparseness about this collection. Unlike *The Letters from a Lady of Quality,* the emphasis in both *La Belle Assemblée* and *L'Entretien* is on love in all its varieties, and each story examines the most universal of emotions from another perspective. Contrary to romance expectations, the majority of the stories explore the theme of persecuted virtue, and they do not have a morally satisfying ending. For example, "The Secret History and Misfortunes of Fatyma" tells of a woman who dies because of her inability to control her aggressive passion for a man, while "The History of Olympia" recounts Olympia's learning to live without a lover, dependent only upon herself.

Facile though they may appear at first glance, these tales provide a valuable lesson for Haywood: that her own stories need not be dependent on happy endings in order to be popular. Although unable to develop her technique of double writing with her translations of Madame de Gomez's works, Haywood was able to perfect her demitragic mode. As apprentice work, these translations gave Haywood the practice that she needed and thus enabled her to concentrate on her own romance plots and develop and polish her technical strategies.

The Lady's Philosopher's Stone

After *La Belle Assemblée*, Haywood translated Louis Adrien Duperron de Castera's *La Pierre philosophale des dames, ou Les Caprices de l'amour et du destin* (1723) as *The Lady's Philosopher's Stone; or, The Caprices of Love and Destiny* (1725).[5] It claims to be a historical novel set during the Cromwellian era in England; instead, it becomes a pastiche of tales delineating the capriciousness of love. Again the focus is on plot rather than techniques, and Haywood abandons herself to the narrative line of the fate of the philosopher's stone.

Love in its Variety

Love in its Variety,[6] her translation of Matteo Bandello's work, is another variation on the theme of ill-placed love. The stories emphasize the arbitrariness of love and the incredibly unhappy state in which women so often find themselves because of this passion.

Women are victimized and exploited by fathers who think they can force love and by suitors who think women do not need love. The tales reinforce the hierarchical order of society that places women in a subservient position to men. Many concern women who are forced into loveless marriages by tyrannical fathers; rather than acquiesce in subservience, they resort to subterfuge, clandestine meetings with lovers, and hasty marriages in order to escape the relationships prescribed for them; in other words, they rebel.

Haywood insinuates her revolutionary notions under cover of Bandello's works. Although her treatment of some of the female characters is unconventional, the stories themselves are quite proper; in each there is a fair mixing of aggressive women who rebel and passive women who accept their fate. The conclusions, however, find the submissive, passive heroines triumphant as they wed and accept their inferior role in the ordered society, while the aggressive females are appropriately punished. Haywood cannot deviate too far from Bandello's text; in her own works, on the other hand, often the rebellious, aggressive woman goes unpunished and the author thus supports her own ideas.

The Disguis'd Prince

Madame de Villedieu's *L'Illustre parisienne* (1679) became Haywood's *The Disguis'd Prince; or, The Beautiful Parisian* (1728).[7] This was the last work she translated during her early period, although *L'Entretien des Beaux Esprits* was done in 1734 as a sequel to *La Belle Assemblée.* (Two other works were translated after an eight-year hiatus.) It is the tale of a prince who weds the beautiful merchant's daughter in spite of many social, political, and moral complications. Since one is virtually assured that the Prince, disguised as Merchant Samuel Solicofane, will eventually win Blanche Bonnin, the novel's lengthy treatment of their adventures and misadventures is tedious in the extreme. There is little character development; both are upright and virtuous at the beginning of the tale and remain so to its end. Its only importance is the practice it afforded Haywood in portraying characters "of a middle state" (1, p. 1), who can be equally as virtuous, elevated, and heroic as the princes and princesses usually found in the pages of romance. The commonplaceness of the characters, however, is more than counterbalanced by the bombast of the speeches. The appearance of this work during the time when Haywood was writing so many works about female distress and persecuted virtue *(The Agreeable Caledonian, Irish Artifice, The Fair Hebrew)* provides assurance that she was vitally aware of the positive effects of impeccable behavior, although she chose to focus here on the more lurid and harsher events of eighteenth-century life.

The Busy-Body

In 1741 and 1742 Haywood returned to translations. After her forced hiatus due to Alexander Pope's attack on her in *The Dunciad,* it was a way for her to put herself in touch once again with popular literary modes and patterns. The first work of this later period was a translation of de Mouhy's *La Mouche, ou Les Aventures et espiègleries facétieuses de Bigand* (1726), which she entitled *The Busy-Body; or, Successful Spy* (1741).[8] The translation is interesting primarily as it is one of two books that Haywood published herself during her short-lived career as a publisher "at the Sign of Fame in Covent Garden." *The Busy-Body* contains the usual adventurous accounts of the rake Bigand's progress, and its sole claim to notoriety in the Haywood canon is that Bigand is the only first-person male narrator to be found in her works. Otherwise, it remains merely a derivative work.

The Virtuous Villager

Her last translation, although it did not recapture the glitter of her earlier works, is far superior to *The Busy-Body*. *The Virtuous Villager; or, Virgin's Victory* (1742)[9] was a translation of Charles de Fieux, Chevalier de Mouhy's *La Paysanne Parvenue*, which was itself adapted from Marivaux's popular *La Vie de Marianne;* Marivaux in turn patterned his work on Richardson's *Pamela*. Both *La Paysanne Parvenue* and *The Virgin's Victory* propound the new "kitchen morality" (a term coined by Whicher to explain the moral lesson of this popular fiction, which sees virtue rewarded for all good, honest servant girls)[10] made popular by *Pamela* and present the themes, tone, and patterns found in Haywood's later novels. It is a story of virtue triumphant, as its title indicates, and, like *The Busy-Body*, is written in the first person. Jeanetta writes that "on my setting down to write these Memoirs of Myself, I intended them as a kind of Mirror, wherein my Sex might view themselves, and perceive by what swift Degrees Errors, if not timely repelled, gain Entrance into the Heart" (p. 5). Like the majority of the novels of the 1750s,[11] it becomes a fictionalized moral tract for the education of young ladies.

Summary

Haywood worked as a translator during key times in her career, and these efforts were instrumental in helping her develop the themes she would explore in her own writing. Learning her trade through her examination of the romances of de Mouhy, Marivaux, and Madame de Gomez, together with her reading of the French novels of de Scudery, la Calprenéde, de Lafayette, and Villedieu, Haywood was able to demonstrate greater control over the romance form than her contemporary novelists; was guaranteed a greater and richer source of ideas, image patterns, and themes; and finally, was able to produce more best-selling romances than her contemporaries and thus achieve financial success. Although she was unable fully to develop and implement her own stylistic strategy that explores woman's parallel reality, the attention she gave to these romances was in general very beneficial to her.

Chapter Six
The Popular Novelist, 1724–1729, Part 1

With the publication in 1724 and 1725 of her collected works, Haywood had achieved a position of prominence that was far more salutary than that attained through her scandalous elopement. Still flagrantly unconventional, however, she began to use her fame and notoriety to sell more novels. From 1724 to 1729 she wrote twenty-nine novels and romances plus numerous translations and nonfictional prose works. Her appetite for work seemed to know no limits, and several times she wrote two or three novels in one month.[1] Understandably, there is great similarity among these tales of passion and intrigue. Virtue in distress is always the theme, although the conclusion is not always the expected and predictable one. Her persecuted heroines do not always conveniently die after their betrayal and seduction; in several instances, they continue to survive independent of the male.

Her successful novels of this period were dependent in large measure on her work in translating continental romances. She was able to learn about popular trends and narrative patterns from them and could adapt these to her advantage by employing new twists and unexpected conclusions that appealed to the sensational taste of her English audience. Unwilling and unable to present her readers with the romantic claptrap they had come to expect from escapist fiction, Haywood, still in the guise of entertainer, tells tales that reveal the startling disproportions of the age: hidden irrational urges that challenge the Age of Reason and exploitation of eighteenth-century women by the men—in general, the discontent and dissatisfaction of the era.

Tentatively at first, Haywood's early novels sought to challenge and test the limits of current philosophy and psychology. The majority of the twenty-nine novels, secret histories, and romances written from 1724 to 1729 forcefully explore human nature, not only its virtuous, public side, but the darker, psychologically repressed, private side. Challenging the accepted belief in the innate goodness of man and the sentimental tenet of good conquering evil, Haywood fed her voracious audience disquieting tales of virtue unrewarded, marriages not made in heaven, physical and mental rape, and female bondage and enslavement.

Only two novels of this period, *The Distressed Orphan* and *Philidore and Placentia,* relate the usual story of the heroine's trials and her reward of marriage to the hero at the conclusion. The rest give a picture of mistreatment and selfish manipulation of the female by the male and the chauvinistic attitudes of society. Nowhere else is Haywood as outspoken as she is here. Couched in intrigue and adventure, the stories tell of victimized and persecuted women who quietly die, and exaggerated, exploited women who clamor for recognition and justice. Reading Haywood's works in their entirety can only lead one to conclude that she is not a mere teller of raucous, titillating tales, but is a careful if unconscious champion of women's rights and position. The initial challenges to the predominant system of order, wit and wisdom, and reason and feeling, found in her six novels of 1719–1723 set the stage for questions into these issues that occupied her thoughts from 1724 to 1729.

The Masqueraders

The first work of this period, *The Masqueraders; or, Fatal Curiosity, parts 1 and 2* (1724–25),[2] is representative of Haywood's entire literary career as she disguises herself and her true intentions within the prolixity of her racy tales. In this work not only is the "charming Rover" Dorimenus (whose real identity is never revealed) disguised, but all of London masquerades in the novel. No one's true nature is revealed, and the whole of human nature is briskly turned upside down.

The novel tells of the philanderings of Dorimenus. "He is young, handsome, gay, gallant, has an affluence of Fortune and of Wit, is a passionate Lover of Intrigue, and 'tis not to be doubted but that with all these Accomplishments, he found a great many among the Fair Sex to encourage that Disposition" (1, p. 6). One such is Dalinda, who "had not Artifice enough to disguise the Pleasure she took in his Conversation" (1, p. 8) and his person. Inevitably, Dorimenus has his way with her. Her physical violation is symptomatic of a larger rape; she had been educated by society to be flighty; she was to be pretty but brainless, interested only in catching a man. Not trained to use her reason, Dalinda exists only to be used, to be taken advantage of and manipulated, and then discarded by the male.

Philecta, the other female protagonist, is quite a different type. She is an example of the non society-trained woman, one who is governed not by her feelings, but by reason. She, too, is very much in love with Dorimenus. Although he continues to press her, Philecta remains firm; she will not become a mere sex object for him. But women, Haywood angrily asserts, are always compromised by men. Even Philecta, "at last, amidst Delight and Pain, a Rack of Extasy on both sides, she more faintly denying, he more vigorously pressing, half yielding, half reluctant . . . was wholly lost,—all her boasted Reason,—all her forceful Resolution,—all the Precautions of so many days, in one tumultuous Moment were overcome" (1, p. 41). Philecta falls victim to the "system"; she is guilty of having taken Dorimenus too seriously. She thought he valued her mind; he only wanted her body, and he is soon enjoying and exploiting both women.

The first part of *The Masqueraders* is a strong indictment of society for its neglect of women's education. Natural, rational tendencies are not trained and strengthened. Although Philecta tries to assert herself and her own identity, it is impossible for her to win against male-dominated odds. At the end, Philecta, now pregnant, is abandoned, and Dorimenus leaves to marry yet another woman, Lysimena.

The patterns of part 1 are repeated in the second half; Dorimenus moves from Lysimena to Briscilla just as he had earlier abandoned Dalinda for Philecta. Briscilla, like Philecta, tries to escape his charms, but in the end she too succumbs and Dorimenus "was at last a conqueror" (2, p. 39) of their bodies and their minds.

At the conclusion, nothing is resolved; Briscilla continues as his mistress; his wife and he hate each other. The story just stops. Haywood challenges the chaos and irrationality that masquerade as order and reason. No longer is virtue rewarded and vice punished, and she looks at the darker side of the human psyche to see why. The world of *The Masqueraders* is a dark one. Vice, greed, and inequality are the ruling elements in this world of male despots and female slaves. The bestial nature is covered over by the veneer of civilization, but Haywood's blunt treatment of Dorimenus's exploits leaves little to the reader's imagination. She strips away the disguise and reveals the beast within the male.

The Fatal Secret

The Fatal Secret; or, Constancy in Distress (1724),[3] Haywood's next novel, continues probing into the demonic interior of the male and investigating the power that drives him totally to enslave, violate, and ultimately kill the defenseless female. In this work, the victim is Anadea, a young maid of sixteen. Initially, she is not quite the routine sort of easily duped heroine; besides being extraordinarily beautiful, she has, even at her age, developed her mind, and "before she arrived at the Age of Sixteen, she acquir'd more than the most ingenious of her Fellow Learners could do at Twenty four. Nor confin'd she her Studies to that part of Education common to her own Sex: she had an extensive Genius, and emulated the other in their Search of Knowledge; she went a great way in the Mathematicks; understood several Languages perfectly well" (p. 208). Since she has been occupied with pursuits of the mind, her social graces have been uncultivated and she has few admirers. Her father, who is afraid to leave her unprovided-for, urges her to consider marriage. Anadea is not interested, but begs her father to "direct me to whom I must resign my Liberty, and I shall yield with a[s] little Reluctance as Nature will permit" (p. 209). The Chevalier de Semar is his choice. Anadea tries dutifully to develop affection for the man, but she remains untouched by true love.

Then one day when she is visiting a friend, she meets the Count de Blessure, and suddenly "the Indifference she had for all Mankind, [was] now converted into the most violent Passion for one" (p. 213). When Blessure learns of her attraction to him, he, too, is overcome with love and begins a campaign to win her away from the prearranged engagement. He persuades Anadea to give up her dutiful suitor and run away with him, and takes her to Versailles, where they are secretly wed. "She was now his own; and she who was hardly brought to make a Break in her Duty to a Parent, would not be guilty of a Sin against it to her Husband: He demanded the full Possession of her Charms the next Night, and the next after that, and so on; she was too obedient to refuse" (p. 231). After a brief interlude the lovers are betrayed by a maid. De Semar hurries to the scene of passion, finds the lovers together, and in the ensuing fight, is killed. Blessure is banished and Anadea is sent to St. Clou, "a Place cut out and fashion'd for Despair" (p. 246). Their marriage remains a secret and precipitates the disastrous events of the conclusion.

While riding in the vicinity of St. Clou, the Marquis de Blessure, her father-in-law, has an accident and is taken to the very inn where Anadea is staying; seeing her, he falls immediately in love with her and presses his suit; he proposes, but Anadea still is true to her husband. The Marquis, unable to control his passionate desires, bribes the maid, drugs Anadea, and rapes her. When the younger Blessure suddenly appears and realizes the full implications of what has just occurred, Anadea "snatched the Sword he wore by his side, and plung'd it in her Bosom" (p. 253). The Marquis shoots himself; his son retires to a Capuchins' monastery and "in wasting Sorrow" (p. 254) dies within three years.

The unexpected incest and bloodbath that conclude *The Fatal Secret* are characteristic of Haywood's rage. Unwilling to write just another soporific account of romantic love, she expands her tale to present her damning commentary on male persecution and female defenselessness. She not only tells a story guaranteed to thrill her audiences, but investigates the reason-passion polemic that governed the age and makes a statement about the condition of women. Clearly, Anadea's fate is one of the most devastating of Haywood's early pieces. The heroine is a mere pawn first exploited by her father, then by Blessure, and then again by his father. Her early inclination to reason is destroyed; she is unacknowledged as a person and becomes the unreal "angel" created by the male. Haywood foregoes double plotting in this novel and does not explore the nature of woman's parallel reality. Rather, she tragically portrays the terrible fate of the typical eighteenth-century woman and gives vent to her extreme anger and frustration.

The Surprise

Her next novel, *The Surprise; or, Constancy Rewarded* (1724),[4] shows the contrary picture. It is the story of Euphemia and Bellamont. Although both are very much in love, Bellamont mysteriously abandons Euphemia on the day of their wedding. The reader subsequently learns that he is too gallant to contract a marriage while deeply in debt. Euphemia, naturally, is shocked, and she falls into a near fatal fever; when she recovers she inherits her rich aunt's estate. Euphemia is not a flighty character, and though she fixes on a plan to save Bellamont, she first tests him to determine whether he has remained faithful to her. Unlike so many of the popular heroines and in contradistinction to women like Anadea, Euphemia becomes the aggressor. Disguised as a courtesan, she tries to seduce Bellamont, but he declines to enter into any sort of illicit union. Highly pleased, Euphemia reveals her identity, pays off his creditors, and weds him. "Thus was *Constancy* on all sides *rewarded;* and by the continu'd Tenderness they had for each other after Marriage, gave a Proof that Possession does not always extinguish desire, and surpris'd the World with an Example, which I am afraid more will *admire* than imitate" (p. 200).

The Surprise lacks the sparkle so often associated with Haywood's tales. Although much of the story is told through the first-person narrative of Euphemia, the prose style is unable to engage the reader's interest, and much of the story remains a rather dull, uninteresting recital of good deeds. Part of the lackluster presentation results also from Haywood's own disbelief in the story she is telling. There are very few fictional heroes of those times like Bellamont who would remain faithful to one woman, would fail to exploit or violate her, and would generally act so unselfishly and humanely. Nor are there women like Euphemia who could so easily gain their objectives in love. In Haywood's world and that of the eighteenth century in general, Bellamont lacks credibility. By making Euphemia an aggressor, Haywood tries to picture the modern woman, but her inadequate psychological study leaves the character underdeveloped.

The Surprise is not a successful novel; Haywood is hemmed in by her plot and cannot give attention to her secondary message. Unable to expose the exploitation and inequality of the female, she loudly praises the constancy and virtuousness of Euphemia and Bellamont, and fails to write a good novel.

The Arragonian Queen

Unlike *The Surprise, The Arragonian Queen: A Secret History* (1724)[5] is a blend of superb character development, good plotting, and the proper amount of action. It is a mixture of heroic adventures in battle (a singular occurrence in Haywood's work) and very involved, amorous intrigues. It deserves special mention because of Zephalinda, the queen, who, like the majority of Haywood's heroines, is used by men. Throughout the first one-third of the novel she is a pawn with no rights of her own: she is the reward promised by her father to the warrior, Albaraizor, if the latter is victorious in the war her father is unsuccessfully waging. Zephalinda is in love with Abdelhamar, "who seem'd . . . to be of superior worth" (p. 5), but she remains faithful to her duty to her father and acquiesces to his demands:

[She is] forc'd into the Arms of a Man she could not love: oblig'd by her Duty to her Father and her virtue, not only to dissemble Inclination where there was nought but cold Indifference, but to stifle the real raging Passion that her bosom glow'd with, and not so much as to indulge her self with a thought of Abdelhamar. (p. 19)

Zephalinda continues in such a state until Abdelhamar returns, when she can no longer contain her love, and "All the tenderness she was beginning to feel for *Albaraizor* was now extinct and vanish'd, and Love, hopeless! unlawful Love for another, with all its Train of wild Perplexities, return'd with greater Force than ever" (p. 42). Only destruction could follow such a passion. Zephalinda arranges for Abdelhamar to marry Selyma, a captive Princess, so he can remain at court. Aware that Abdelhamar is unable to have true affection for her, Selyma jealously spreads wicked tales about him and Zephalinda and persuades Albaraizor that his wife is unfaithful. An intercepted, indiscreet letter from Abdelhamar confirms these suspicions, and Albaraizor has both Zephalinda and Abdelhamar banished and put into prison. *The Arragonian Queen* becomes a commentary on the wages of passion for a woman who loves neither too wisely nor too well.

Zephalinda frustrates the reader. Selyma, however, is a very satisfying character, functioning as the symbol of Haywood's rage. Selyma's cry to Abdelhamar is a revelation of the utmost anger: "confusion sieze thee . . . to whom do I owe my Servitude, and demeaning of my State beneath that of Zephalinda, but to thee! Unworthy and insulting as thou art! was I not born a Princess. . . . Was I not bred to equal Hopes, till thou, Destroyer, laid'st my Country waste . . . and brought myself a Captive to Valencia" (p. 51). Selyma, too, has been made into an object to be used by the male; her anger and revenge are expressions of Haywood's feelings.

Women can never win, it would appear, and Haywood cannot, will not accept such a fate; through Selyma she expresses her wrath. The remainder of *The Arragonian Queen* is Haywood's overt statement about the oppression of women.

Fantomina and *The City Jilt*

Haywood's statement made through the characters of Zephalinda and Selyma describes her frustration and anger at the female plight and forms the focal point of several other novels from her first, major productive period. Almost in direct answer to *The Arragonian Queen* are *Fantomina; or, Love in a Maze* (1724)[6] and *The City Jilt; or, The Alderman Turn'd Beau* (1726),[7] two works that depict in great detail the aggressive woman who takes control.

As *Fantomina* begins, the reader is introduced to a young lady of beauty, wit, and spirit, who, suddenly free from parental guidance and control, decides to exercise her own will. Long interested in the rogue Beauplaisir and intrigued by his reputation as a lady-killer, she disguises herself as the courtesan Fantomina and begins an intrigue with him. Initially, she resolves "to receive his Devoirs as a Town-Mistress, imagining a world of Satisfaction to herself in engaging him in the Character of such a one, and in observing the Surprise he would be in to find himself refused by a Woman, who he supposed granted her Favours without Exception" (pp. 260–61) and certainly one whom he could easily control. Unfortunately for Fantomina, such is not the case, and she is quite easily caught in his sexual trap and is "undone" (p. 263). She is not an Anadea; she revolts as much as is possible for her to do. When Beauplaisir tires of her and casts her off, Fantomina takes on the disguise of Celia the chambermaid and captures his attentions once again. This pattern is repeated twice more, with Fantomina becoming the Widow Bloomer and Incognita, the Lady of Quality. Beauplaisir never discovers her duplicity, and for a time Fantomina, the supposedly weak female, dominates.

Not only does she satisfy her own sexual inclinations, she smugly believes that "while he thinks to fool me, [he] is himself the only beguiled Person" (p. 277). But nature outsmarts them both. Fantomina discovers that she is pregnant and her mother packs her off to a convent in France to have her baby. There the story ends, but not before Haywood has had a chance to explore male/female power structures. Haywood brings her usually hidden tale of female domination to the surface as she constructs her story around Fantomina's supposed control of Beauplaisir. The structure proves inadequate, as Haywood undercuts the story with Fantomina's final loss of power. Overt and covert meanings merge and women's parallel reality is revealed, at least in this instance, as a sham; Beauplaisir goes unpunished. Women cannot hope to succeed if their only hope of control is sex.

Similarly, in *The City Jilt* Haywood creates an aggressive spokeswoman for her own feelings. Glicera is first violated by the male, but is able ultimately to triumph.

On the eve of her wedding, Glicera's father dies, and she must quickly change her bridal clothes for mourning. Her beloved Melladore's affections change with her attire, and soon his "nobler Inclinations" are gone and "brutal Appetite alone remained" (p. 7). He dissembles and masks his lust with bland words and harmless actions, and Glicera, subdued at last, falls "the Victim of his lawless Flame" (p. 7). Predictably, in a short time, Melladore's passion cools and Glicera discovers that she is pregnant. He discards her, assuming she will retreat to the country, and he marries the rich Helena.

Glicera, however, will not quietly retire from the London scene, but determines to work her own revenge on her perjured lover. The "Memory of her Wrongs . . . left her not a Moment, and by degrees settled so implacable a hatred in her nature, not only to *Melladore,* but to that whole undoing Sex, that she never rejoyc'd so much as when she heard of the Misfortune of any of them" (p. 20). To secure her revenge, she determines to gain control of Melladore's land; to this end she tantalizes and teases Alderman Grubguard, Melladore's agent. Soon she learns that because Helena is in fact illegitimate and her inheritance worthless, Melladore has lost his entire estate and is forced to mortgage it to Grubguard. Glicera gets control of the mortgage and then discards Grubguard. She has achieved her aim: Melladore is forced to beg enough money from her to purchase a commission in the army, in whose service he is subsequently killed. Glicera does not stop with Melladore, for "the Hatred which [Melladore's] Ingratitude had created in her Mind was so fix'd and rooted there, that it became a part of her Nature, and she seem'd born only to give Torment to the whole Race of Man, nor did she know another Joy in Life" (p. 29). After collecting a large sum from her scorned lovers, she retires to the country, and "tho' Her Hatred ceas'd[,] she persever'd in her Resolution, never to forgive the Treatment she had received" (p. 59) from Melladore.

The City Jilt is a damning commentary on the eighteenth-century axiom of virtue rewarded. Glicera's initial, virtuous reception of Melladore is scorned and flaunted; her chaste and naive acceptance of him as a lover is not recognized, and she is soon scorned and cast aside. Glicera is another personification of Haywood's hatred of men. Haywood challenges her women readers to feel the same. There is no reason they must be acquiescent to the will of men, and in The City Jilt she says exactly what they can do as she describes a woman in control sexually, socially, and economically.

The Force of Nature, The Unequal Conflict, and The Fatal Fondness

Unfortunately, Fantominas and Gliceras are exceptions in Haywood's novels rather than the rule. The majority of the works in this 1724–1729 period present women who are harassed, exploited, and victimized by men. More than their individual struggles, it is the sheer number and bulk of these heroines that must be noted. Haywood moves from controlled women—The Force of Nature and The Unequal Conflict and its sequel The Fatal Fondness—to those who not only are dominated but are destroyed—The Mercenary Lover and The Double Marriage. Only two works of this period, The Distressed Orphan and Philidore and Placentia (see Chapter 7) offer a positive ending to this disastrous state of feminine affairs; only two offer the panacea of marriage; for the rest, life is a continuous battle with the woman always as victim.

Felisinda of The Force of Nature; or, The Lucky Disappointment (1724)[8] is an archetypal pawn in the games the controlling men play. Her father, Don Alvario, refuses to allow her to marry her beloved Fernando and instead arranges a union with Don Carlos. Felisinda, displaying some spirit, not only rejects Don Carlos and his attentions, but more important, she refuses to let her father consider her a mere sex object. She tells him so, and for her efforts is sent to the monastery of the Augustines.

Try as she might, Felisinda cannot exercise her own will. Even when she thinks she has found a friend and confidante in Alantha, she is duped. Alantha was only using Felisinda to get to Fernando, with whom she had fallen in love. More plot complications arise, each portion another link that fetters Felisinda to the male will more securely. Even Alantha is caught, as she is abducted and almost raped. At the end, only the Abbess Berenthia can untangle the intricacies of the plot: Fernando is her son; his father was Don Alvario. (Her revelations are made in an effort to stop the possible incest.) Since Fernando cannot now marry Felisinda, he turns to Alantha, who is overcome with joy; Felisinda is left with Don Carlos. Incest has been avoided, and one can only imagine that Felisinda will be content; certainly, if she continues to submit to male authority, she cannot but succeed according to male rules and fail horribly by female standards.

Similarly, in *The Unequal Conflict* (1725)[9] and *The Fatal Fondness* (1725)[10] Haywood shows the effects of a woman's being a pawn in men's game of life. The former is important because it is her first novel that deals at some length with the unredeeming, calamitous effects of love. Virtue is not rescued or rewarded but is persecuted; love is exploited, not saved. Unlike *The Force of Nature, The Unequal Conflict* does not try to camouflage the usual fate of the eighteenth-century woman; instead it explicitly examines man's manipulation and torture of the female.

As the story begins, Philenia, the darling of her parents, is engaged to Coeurdemont but falls in love with the penniless Fillamour. Her father becomes angry, "ordering her to retire to her chamber, made her be confin'd therein; solemnly vowing not to restore her liberty, till she consented to his will, in marrying the person he knew to be most worthy of her" (p. 10). Marriage to Coeurdemont looks to be her only means of escape. Philenia grows desperate, but her friend Antonia offers hope, and together they plan how to break out of her prison.

In her novels and romances preceding *The Unequal Conflict*, Haywood did not investigate friendship among women to any extent; instead, women were negligent of each other or behaved odiously toward their own sex. With Antonia as her spokeswoman, Haywood examines the relationships of women to women, to the romance tradition, to fiction, and to men. Antonia tries to help Philenia, and in her role as spokeswoman for Haywood, she does so in an imaginative, creative way. For the first time, the woman tries to control the plot, not the man. As Barbara Bellow Watson outlined, with Antonia, it is a question of power, of who has it and how it is used *(Signs,* I). Specifically, Antonia/Haywood creates a romance fiction about Fillamour and Philenia, remarking that "the Knight of the afflicted heart will soon find a way to free the damsel from the enchanted castle" (p. 15). Antonia plots a romantic abduction in which "Philenia's Lover, accompanied by his two servants, all disguis'd and mask'd" (p. 22) will enter the house and forcibly abduct her. Antonia openly flaunts parental authority and the submission expected of a woman; she shows how women can control man and his carefully orchestrated but, as regards women, inhumane plans. Through Antonia and her actions, Haywood exposes her anger at the female condition, yet she only succeeds in emphasizing the women's fetters. Philenia merely moves from one sort of bondage to another, while in the final analysis, Antonia demonstrates her lack of total freedom from the male. Although Antonia tries to control the male (and thereby help her friend), that she abducts and seduces Philenia merely emphasizes her enslavement to the male conventions. She attempts to free Philenia from parental fetters, but she merely confines her further within manmade boundaries; at the last, Philenia remains a battered heroine.

Surprisingly enough, Antonia's abduction plot is successful, but not the rest of her plans. Like Haywood, she is foiled by exterior society. For example, she learns that if Fillamour marries Philenia, he faces financial ruin, for his uncle has arranged a wealthier match for him. Philenia, innocent that she is, agrees to postpone their marriage and maintain "a *Platonick* passion" (p. 57) toward him for a while; she returns to her father's house and learns of Fillamour's marriage. Only in Antonia's romantic fabrication would Fillamour have waited for Philenia; in reality, he could not "throw off the nature of his sex, forget he was a man" (p. 57) and reject the wealthiest, most accessible woman. Fillamour is typical of the male sex: as far as Haywood is concerned, he is a cad. He both enjoys his wife and finds time and the opportunity to meet Philenia again. He rapes her. There is no peace for Philenia, and soon after the rape, she is abducted by a band of villains and further victimized.

Antonia, too, fails in her role as woman saver, power controller, and creator. Unable to shape her friend's life as she chooses, she is faced with a disastrous sequel to her original, well-thought-out story. She is saved from one disastrous relationship only to be plunged into far worse circumstances created by Haywood in an effort to mirror, in metaphor, the true situation of women.

In volume 2, *The Fatal Fondness,* Philenia has been saved from her ravishers by a timely shipwreck and has spent the intervening year in a fishing village. She is found and returned to the city by Antonia and Coeurdemont, who have been married for some time. Philenia returns only to find Fillamour lying in his own blood, stabbed by a jealous lover. Philenia stabs herself and dies, but Fillamour recovers to live a life of undying remorse and grief.

The story operates on several levels. The first obviously concerns Haywood's frustration at the exploitation of women and heroines like Philenia. It is also an outline, albeit rough, of her own combat, of her own aggressive plan of revenge that she tries to implement through her fiction. Haywood depicts the parallel reality of women by means of the story of Philenia and Antonia. She also explores the issue of feminine power and control through Antonia's attempts to change reality with plots and fabrications of her own. But all such endeavors fail. Antonia cannot change or even mask the sad reality that sees women like Philenia further harassed by men. Perhaps Haywood's inability to deal with this reality at this point in her career also explains the plot of *The Fatal Fondness.* Antonia's reward, a partially successful marriage, reveals a slight hesitancy on Haywood's part to give a total endorsement to such manipulative, aggressive behavior. Antonia becomes less and less forceful, finally existing merely as a figurehead, while Philenia remains, like the majority of Haywood's women, a paradigm of exploitation.

The Distressed Orphan, The Mercenary Lover, and *The Double Marriage*

In Haywood's next novels, *The Distressed Orphan; or, Love in a Madhouse* (1726), *The Mercenary Lover; or, the Unfortunate Heiresses* (1726) and *The Double Marriage; or, the Fatal Release* (1726), she continues to investigate this theme. She does not try to create any more spokeswomen such as Antonia, and instead relies on the techniques of plot and setting to comment on women's situation.

The Distressed Orphan[11] is the story of the beautiful Annilia, who "had the misfortune to lose both her parents before she arrived at an age capable of knowing what it was to be an orphan" (p. 3). She is cared for by Giraldo, her uncle, who seeks to control her fortune; he promotes a match between her and his son, Horatio, and initially, she acquiesces. When she meets Colonel Marathon at a ball, looking "on him as something divine" (p. 9), she immediately falls in love with him; "the sight of Horatio was now grown poison to her eyes, and nothing troubled her so much, as that she had given him hope of being his" (p. 15). Annilia is learning the arts of survival, however, and "love had now taught her the art of disguising her sentiments" (p. 15), and unlike Philenia, she creates subterfuges for her survival. She demands her "liberty" until she is "restrained" by marriage. In the meantime, she discovers Uncle Giraldo's cupidity and becomes cautious about revealing her relationship with Marathon. Unfortunately, she is not careful enough. When Giraldo learns of her new affection, he imprisons her in the house and tells everyone that Annilia was "seized with a most violent frenzy" (p. 28); her only way to freedom, he tells her, is marriage to Horatio.

Since Annilia will not comply, Giraldo has her carried off in "the dead of night" (p. 32) to an asylum, and "Like a lamb among a herd of wolves, she was seized by these inhuman ruffians" (p. 32). Marathon's love proves to be strong and cannot be stopped by locked doors, barred windows, and supposed insanity. Disguising himself as Lovemore and counterfeiting madness himself, he gains entrance to the asylum and rescues Annilia; they escape and marry. Giraldo dies soon afterward of a fever, and Horatio is exiled.

Not until Charlotte Smith's *The Young Philosopher* (1798) and Mary Wollstonecraft's *Maria; or, The Wrongs of Women* (1798) will such a piece of literature be so vitally set in a madhouse. In all three novels, the asylum functions as a symbolic matrix for the authors' statements about the fate of women, that is, imprisonment mirrors both their physical and mental fetters. In *The Distressed Orphan,* Haywood does not resort to complex strategy, but frankly and boldly describes the actual fate of the majority of women.

Haywood, however, plays on the romantic tastes of her public and creates a happy ending for Annilia and Colonel Marathon, but such deference does not totally compromise or destroy the brutal frankness of the rest of the tale. Although she dilutes the ferocious impact of her own anger with this ending, earlier scenes clearly establish the horror of women's fate. Annilia does not have to die to be its symbol.

Haywood continues in *The Mercenary Lover*[12] to explore the crimes that male villains perpetrate on unsuspecting and naive females. Blacker than Annilia's Uncle Giraldo, Clitander is the personification of the seducer, the violator of innocence.

Initially, however, he is shown in a favorable light; of all Miranda's suitors, "he alone had the Power of Inspiring her with a real Passion" (p. 10), and Miranda soon discards her coquetry and marries him: "they were look'd on by all who knew them, as the most exemplary Patterns of Conjugal Affection" (p. 11). All this is facade, and becomes emblematic of the great disparity between appearance and reality throughout the novel.

Clitander is the worst villain/deceiver to be found in these early novels. "Money was the only Darling of his mercenary Wishes" (p. 12); to get as much of it as possible, he plans on jilting the two sisters, Miranda and Althea, out of their substantial inheritance. He marries the more frivolous Miranda and immediately begins to plot how to seduce the older girl. Flattering speeches and solicitous behavior soon win her over because her mind, like Miranda's, is not educated to detect the false notes of a deceiving man. Althea is so hoodwinked that even when she discovers her pregnancy and Clitander's falseness, she will not see him in his true colors—"I confess the Prevalence of thy too fatal Charms, and once more own myself all thine" (p. 48). But mental and physical possession is not enough for him; Clitander will stop at nothing until her property and inheritance are his as well. When he tries to violate even that portion of her that is earmarked for her offspring, Althea at last begins to suspect him; amid her tears and ravings, Clitander momentarily loses his ability to deceive her. His final act of poisoning her is anticlimatic, for when she accepts him again, which she had done prior to taking the poison, she truly condemns herself to death. Nothing less than the total destruction of this woman, mind and body, is displayed here in explicit terms. Haywood does not employ the double writing used in other tales; here she openly castigates the male for his physical and psychological rape of the female.

Riding the crest of her popularity, Haywood was able to create exceptionally atypical heroines during this period. Although she was anxious to present her revolutionary doctrine of women's freedom quietly and covertly, she wanted also to express her own anger and frustration, and she does so in such characters as Glicera, Althea, and Fantomina. Clearly, Haywood is aware that she cannot single-handedly change the focus and direction of the literary scene, but she can try to stem the tide of female subservience by educating her readers to their state.

With *The Double Marriage,*[13] Haywood turns again to this revolutionary notion. The story begins tamely enough. From their childhood, Bellcour and Alathia have been lovers, and "As their Years
encreased, so did their mutual Ardors. . . . *Bellcour,* as it was the
Business of his Sex, first declar'd the passionate Wishes of his en-
amour'd Soul, which *Alathia* receiv'd with a modest Contentment
in her Eyes" (p. 3). It is just such sex roles that Haywood upsets,
and in the course of the story she shakes her readers from complacent
acceptance of this stereotyping.

Alathea agrees to wed Bellcour in secret, but their brief interlude
of marital bliss is soon interrupted when Bellcour learns that his
father has arranged a marriage for him to a wealthy Indian heiress,
Mirtamene. Bellcour possesses none of the determination and challenge found in other heroes, and he soon finds himself caught in
his father's snare: literally, he is kidnapped.

Bellcour is an ambivalent hero at best. Although unwilling to
champion and fight for the woman he loves, he rushes to the rescue
like a typical hero when he hears of an unknown maiden who is
being tortured by "a Man well habited, but with a Devil-like Fierce-
ness in his Countenance" (p. 38). Naturally, this woman turns out
to be Mirtamene. Bellcour is so smitten with her beauty that "All
that Resolution, which Tenderness he had bourne Alathia had inspired him with, vanish'd" (p. 53), and with one last thought for
his wife, he agrees to marry Mirtamene.

Meanwhile, Alathea has heard rumors of Bellcour's behavior and,
unable to settle her feelings with rational explanations, disguises
herself as a boy and goes off in search of the truth. She confronts
Bellcour and is so overwhelmed at his perfidy and faithlessness that
she stabs herself. Bellcour, seeing "the Woman whom he had once
lov'd, with an extremity of ardor breathing her last, through his
Ingratitude and Perjury. . . and on the other, the deceived *Mirtamene* with, even in ignorance, Reproaches in her Eyes" (p. 60),
totally gives way to his feelings; he stabs himself and dies.

Only Mirtamene survives. Thus "warn'd by the Example of Bellcour, that Interest, Absence, or a new Passion, can make the most
seeming constant lover false, [she] took a Resolution ever to condemn
and hate that betraying Sex to which she owed his Misfortune and
the Sight of such a Disaster as she had beheld in Alathia" (p. 61).
Mirtamene learns to see correctly. She is made aware of the parallel
reality that exists below the other reality, the deception perpetrated

by the male; she learns to unite her passion and reason and, presumably, goes on to lead a more prudently governed life. Thus Mirtamene ends where other, more aggressive women have also been. Fantomina, Glicera, and Antonia have indicated the path that can and should be taken. Mirtamene is left to put such lessons into practice.

Memoirs of a Certain Island, Bath Intrigues, and The Court of Carimania

Haywood also tried her hand at the popular roman à clef. *The Arragonian Queen,* for example, is subtitled *A Secret History,* but in such works as *Memoirs of a Certain Island Adjacent to the Kingdom of Utopia* (1725),[14] *Bath Intrigues: in four Letters to a Friend in London* (1725),[15] *Memoirs of the Baron de Brosse* (1724),[16] *The Secret History of the Present Intrigues of the Court of Carimania* (1726),[17] and *Letters from the Palace of Fame* (1727),[18] she fully exploits the *chronique scandalouse* (scandal novel) popularized by Delariviere Manley in *The New Atalantis* (1709).

These works differ from the romances in their demanding attention to detail, with portraits so particularized that Haywood's inclusion of a "key" to identify Romanus, Davilla, or Flirtillaria seems almost redundant. When considered in terms of novel development, however, this detail is sketchy at best; the characters have little depth or psychological intensity, and they overwhelm the reader not by great individuality but by sheer bulk.

In the *Memoirs,* Haywood creates a virtual cavalcade of caddish men and aggressively vampish women. There are few good characters; the majority are polluted, diseased, decayed, and distorted; examples of worthless love, inconstancy, perjury, and discord. Men are rapists who violate women and order; women are aggressors who violate men and their rightful position in society. Volume 1 is set in the country and is concerned primarily with evil, unruly, aggressive women; volume 2 takes place in the city, specifically amid the life of the court and the palace, and focuses on men.

In the first volume the aggressive female is presented, in most instances, with an almost artless, fairy-tale simplicity. Flirtillaria, for example, as her name implies, trifles with love and men; "in her [are] Extremes of Good and Evil—there is no Virtue she is not capable of—nor scarce, Vice she does not Practice" (1, p. 34).

Ultimately, it is the uncontrolled side of evil, passion, and avarice that rules, and like her soulmate, Gloatitia, Flirtillaria brings destruction to all males with whom she is in contact, thus becoming contemptible to the world. Next there is Clarismonda: this "fair Apostate is scarce nineteen, yet she is mistress of more artifice than half her Sex beside" (1, p. 49). The Duchess is a real sorceress; initially a prostitute, she quickly becomes the "most haughty and impervious wife" (1, p. 61) to the Duke. A lustful, shrewish woman, the Duchess has numerous affairs, seducing each male with whom she comes in contact. One of these is the naive Windusius, and when her passion for him cools, she chooses to ruin him rather than just cast him aside. This liaison is only a preliminary to Windusius's major affair with Wyaria, the "false fair," who with her great "Foulness of Soul" (1, p. 109) becomes the aggressive wooer and comes to his bed also to engineer his undoing. At the end, Wyaria chooses an incestuous life with her brother-in-law, and Windusius is discarded again. These portions of the *Memoirs* are Haywood's actualizations of her own aggressive wishes and desires; the male is manipulated and punished for his earlier treatment of women.

The aggressive women in the first volume—numerous others could be listed—are out to rape the male and survive as wantonly as they can. To include so many, all barely distinguishable, suggests the ubiquitous nature of female exploitation. Haywood's feelings are barely contained; there is no sophisticated approach dallying between overt and covert tales. Almost immediately, she ceases to be concerned with the *chronique scandalouse* and turns furiously to displaying the total degradation to which women are subject.

The second volume further depicts decay and sinful existence, this time principally through an endless roll call of rakes and libertines. Ricardo, the "Slave of Lust" (2, p. 125), rapes Bellyra and abandons her; Silvander rapes Plaisira and then tells her he is already married; Rufilius undoes the country wife of the tradesman; Corruvanus leaves his intended at the altar in hopes of making a more lucrative match; Argaspe drugs and rapes Lamira and abandons her and his child. The "Island adjacent to the Kingdom of Utopia" is oppressed with the weight of sin and shame. Rape is the only action described in this novel. All order is violated; separation, alienation, and disintegration reign supreme.

Memoirs of a Certain Island is Haywood's attempt to confront hardcore, female subjugation and to portray the age as she sees it.

Bath Intrigues, another roman à clef, is her further attempt to expose this inequality through extraordinary exaggeration. Discarding any attempt at subtle expression, she paints a very nasty picture of her society. She writes to reclaim "this blissful Spot of Earth" that "no more shall groan beneath the oppressive Weight of Sin and Shame" (2, p. 276); she writes to uncover the rankness in the garden so that it can become a pleasure spot once again. Haywood clearly poses, creating works that become more and more believable in an effort to underscore the ubiquitous, pernicious effects of being untrue to oneself, of allowing men to dominate women.

The use of the epistolary form seemingly gives *Bath Intrigues* more impact than the *Memoirs;* not only is Haywood able to catch up her readers in the immediacy of letters, she can examine the female psyche. In general, though, her sketches are cursory and merely furnish the reader with summary versions of the forms and models she used before. For example, we read about Amanda, a dutiful wife, whose husband is repeatedly unfaithful to her. She tries to reclaim his affections by making him jealous. When her affair with Cleanthus is discovered, she is "condemn'd as the most criminal Woman on Earth" (p. 20). Haywood's message is clear: a woman must suffer all sorts of inhumanities, but she is not permitted to act in kind. Sexual coercion, force, threats, and blackmail are the tools and techniques of the male; nowhere else is Haywood so blunt in her exposure of such tactics.

With *The Secret History of the Present Intrigues of the Court of Carimania* Haywood avoids the crowded, exaggerated scene and confines herself to recounting the sordid amours carried on by Theodore, Prince of Carimania, with various beauties of the court. She minutely chronicles his rogue's progress as he woos, seduces, enjoys, and casts off mistresses too numerous to mention. *The Secret History* is, in reality, a thinly disguised portrait of the English court: Prince Theodore is George II; Hyanthe is his wife, Queen Caroline; the luscious Ismonda, Theodore's mistress, is Mrs. Henrietta Howard; and Adrastus, Ismonda's husband, is Colonel Howard. Haywood's blunt characterizations, coupled with Pope's defamation of her in *The Dunciad,* resulted in her subsequent literary ostracism and a seeming ten-year silence. (In point of fact, only four years were totally silent.) Contemporary judgment was harsh; fortunately, reaction was delayed and 1727 was a very good year for her. Although Haywood most certainly did expose the scandalous behavior of the court, if one looks at the work more closely, one can see that it follows the patterns she had already established by exposing the male myth that had seduced so many women and describing the female reality that exists underneath this falsehood. Prince Theodore's exploits are no more reprehensible than those of Giraldo and other villains in Haywood's canon. Of course, time has given the contemporary reader the perspective that was lacking in 1726, but it is unfortunate that one of the most important voices of the age was temporarily silenced because of her passion for truth.

Like the *Memoirs of a Certain Island, The Court of Carimania* succeeds by exaggeration, by presenting everything in extremes. There is absolutely no freedom for women. The few who attempt to control are, in the final reality, still encompassed by men and their desires and manipulations. The satire of both works is biting; Haywood does not offer much hope for women's salvation. Of course, the whole thrust of a satiric piece is to present reality in extremes, but Haywood tries to connect this notion with her own technique of double writing. Neither work succeeds as admirably as her novels and romances.

Summary

One can note Haywood's increasing ease with the novel form; never content merely to reproduce a story that had existed previously, she is always at pains to present just enough of a different focus to make the tale viable for her own purpose. She continues to probe women's elusive other reality; in an effort to interest new readers, in novels like *The Force of Nature, The Unequal Conflict,* and *Fatal Fondness* she offers seemingly straightforward stories of sex and titillation. Underneath, she continues to display the sexual harassment of the female.

Chapter Seven
The Popular Novelist, 1724–1729, Part 2

Haywood's popularity continued, with 1727 especially notable because of the publication of *Philidore and Placentia,* perhaps the single most important novel of these years. This period further witnessed increased sophistication in her art; her presentation of woman's double reality was honed to a fine point, while she continued to perfect the depiction of her aggressive avatars. Several of the works between 1724 and 1729 appear to be extensions (revisions, perhaps) of earlier pieces (e.g., *The Perplex'd Dutchess* follows from *The City Jilt*), but rather than appearing merely repetitive, they indicate the great importance Haywood attached to her argument about women's rights and position. Furthermore, these works show her increasing concern with the mechanics of writing fiction; there is more attention paid to the art of creating. Haywood seems aware of the power of the written word and is now ready to use it.

Cleomelia

With *Cleomelia; or, the Generous Mistress* (1727),[1] Haywood returned to the complicated, often exaggerated plot that had become her stock in trade, but besides the usual inanity, she attempted to reveal her own increasing interest in writing fiction.

As the story begins, Cleomelia has secretly engaged herself to Gaspar, and at fourteen has already become an inveterate liar. Her fabrications are so good that her father, believing his daughter's affections unattached, arranges her marriage to young Heartlove. Not only does Cleomelia play the hypocrite, but from the start she retains control of the situation, although, unlike Fantomina, Glicera, Selyma, and Ismonda, it is of short duration, and the power reverts to the male.

Cleomelia continues to dissemble and soon has Heartlove and her father convinced of her sincere affection for the suitor but also of

her inability to wed him. Heartlove is stricken to his very soul, but
he releases Cleomelia from her bond. To this point, the overt and
covert stories are combined as the female is in control; for a while,
at least, the male is forced to conform to her dictates. Such a situation
is a momentary delusion. When Cleomelia discovers she is pregnant,
both Gaspar and her father agree that a proper marriage must take
place. Gaspar's father is adamant in his refusal to bless their union,
and secretly he kidnaps his son and ships the lad off to the continent.
Gaspar's best friend, Favonius, creates an elaborate story about Gaspar's sudden departure and convinces Cleomelia and her father that
she has been deserted. Her father suddenly dies, and Cleomelia,
"her Reputation lost, her Virtue taint'd . . . fell into a Despair"
(p. 35). She also loses her ability to command. Now in control,
Heartlove demonstrates his heroic quality and offers to marry her.

Their bliss is soon interrupted by a letter from Gaspar in which
he declares and vows his still faithful love for Cleomelia. Unable to
face either Gaspar or Heartlove and choose between them, Cleomelia
boards a ship for England; en route, amid tremendous storms, the
ship's captain proposes to her; nowhere it seems, can Cleomelia be
free from men and their importunings. When she receives word
that Heartlove has been killed in a duel with Gaspar, she marries
the captain; unable to rule completely, she settles for being controlled. Evaluating her state, she observes, "Wretched *Cleomelia,*
how has thou undone, and how art thou thyself undone!" (p. 61).

Ever-faithful Gaspar returns once again to claim her, only to find
Cleomelia wed a second time. He leaves in despair and heads for
England; when her second husband is lost at sea, Cleomelia also
goes to England and at last rewards Gaspar and marries him. Virtue
is rewarded, if rather haphazardly.

Cleomelia is a long and intricately plotted novel from Haywood's
middle period. There is an excessive amount of tedious "and then,"
"and then" narration about it. Initially, Haywood seems to have
constructed the novel as a creative exercise. The many stories, rumors, and falsehoods that circulate throughout, used both as in-
centive and hindrance to the plot action, reveal Haywood's attempt
to flex her literary muscles. But all the characters become trapped,
and Haywood herself soon is lost in complexities of the plot. There
is little attempt to search beneath the exterior and examine characters' motivations, and although her notion of fiction making in

the novel is important, *Cleomelia* is not as successful as other novels from this period.

Haywood continues to be fascinated with prevarication as a means to control power and will return to it in other novels, especially those of her later years, *The History of Miss Betsy Thoughtless* and *The History of Jemmy and Jenny Jessamy.* There, she examines the relationship between fiction and reality, between appearance and reality. The protagonists learn that they cannot view the world through the appearance-oriented spectacles of romance. [2]

In *Cleomelia,* however, Haywood is not ready to make such an assessment. Cleomelia makes up romantic escapades because she thinks that they enable her to exert feminine power over men. It is a situation analagous to Haywood's own. She, as creator, controls through her writings; unlike Cleomelia, she reveals the reality and truth beneath the tales of fantasy concocted by the protagonists. Haywood's real power is demonstrated in her hidden stories, which in *Cleomelia,* as in much of her early fiction, details woman's exploitation, imprisonment, and manipulation by men. Cleomelia thinks she controls, but the truth, as revealed in the interior tale, is quite the reverse. Gaspar and Philidore, it must be noted, are the noteworthy exceptions to these evaluations about the male and his creations.

The Fruitless Enquiry

The Fruitless Enquiry (1727)[3] is a series of adventures and misadventures of Miramillia, the widow of a nobleman of Venice who has lost her only son and can only regain him, she has been told, when she has a shirt made for him by a woman who is perfectly content. [4] Haywood writes in the dedication that the tales are designed by the author to "persuade my Sex from seeking Happiness the wrong Way," while Mrs. Griffith, the editor of *A Collection of Novels* in which *The Fruitless Enquiry* appeared, remarks that the piece is intended "to abate envy, and conciliate content; by shewing, in a variety of instances, that appearances are frequently fallacious; that perfect or permanent happiness is not the lot of mortal life; and that peace of mind, and rational enjoyment are only to be found in bosoms free from guilt" (p. 162). Perspicaciously, she has observed the impulse that makes Haywood's work so important in the history of women's literature when she notes the author's concern with appearance and reality. Even though the collection of short stories is not extraordinarily brilliant, and at times is downright dull, Haywood is still careful to employ the rhetorical strategy that details the double reality, the actual situation as dictated by the male and the psychological condition as experienced by the female. Haywood emphasizes female suffering as she recounts tale after tale (too numerous to mention here) of women duped, violated, and left to die by men.

Yes, Haywood would assert, women are wretched and disquieted by their lives. Men, who have devised and created the real world, would have them believe differently although this would result in a delusion of ease, dependence, and happy servitude. In The *Fruitless Enquiry,* as she has done in all her novels, Haywood endeavors to strip away this facade and reveal the devastating reality of female enslavement and exploitation that lies below.

"The History of Anziana" is the best example of this concept and of Haywood's skills. The story begins with Miramillia's discovery of a literal skeleton "of a man, with arms extended wide, as if in an act to seize the adventurous gazer" (p. 168) in Anziana's closet. Affixed to his chest, is the label: "Remember, Anziana, it is for your crime that I am thus; and let a just contrition take up your ensuing days, and peace be ever a stranger to your soul, till you become as I am" (p. 168). Inevitably, the reader is impelled to read on to discover the explanation of this phenomenon. Haywood has Anziana tell her own story, thus enabling the reader to view the myth of female persecution at first hand. The covert tale thus becomes the surface story.

Anziana confesses that as a child she was raised not to use her reason. When her father is rescued from great financial difficulties by Caprera and offers Anziana to the man in payment, she cannot forget Lorenzo, with whom she is desperately in love. In her imagination she pictures the real miseries she would have to endure should she refuse to obey her father, and therefore she agrees to the marriage. Because she has no skills of logic, she must glibly accept the supposed rational notion of the male.

Lest one become involved in the plot only, Haywood judiciously inserts lessons in how to read her story so that a person can see the difference between the obvious and hidden messages. This is one of the few places in the Haywood oeuvre in which she actually directs the reader. Just as Anziana reverses her decision and determines to go to Lorenzo, a little French novel, *L'Inconstance d'amours,* falls on her head. "It contained several little histories of the ingratitude of mankind, and the little they thought themselves obliged, even from the greatest condescensions our sex could make: I looked on this accident as a kind of warning to me . . . and . . . began to read it; where the first story I happened to cast my eyes on, was a kind of parallel with my own; it being of a young lady who had forsook her father, friends, and country, for the dear sake of love" (p. 176). Predictably, the woman of the tale is jilted. Haywood's intention is clear: her own readers must learn from Anziana's plight as Anziana learns from the French novel. Haywood's method is simple, yet the more subtle technique of her double writing is also evident as one recalls that Anziana is narrating her story to Miramillia; Anziana is creating a second level that comments on and uncovers the first story and attempts to divulge still further the true state of women's existence. When Lorenzo asks Anziana to prostitute herself to him, she strips away his mask and reveals his lecherous soul. The letters that they exchange promulgate more lies than those of the little French novel. Anziana's remark, "pretend not to be what you are not, nor imagine I do so" (p. 184) is prophetic, for the entire story is based on living a lie, pretending to be something other than what one is. All the characters are disguised: Anziana hides her true nature and agrees to love a man she cannot; her father and husband disguise themselves in forged letters in order to catch her in her intrigue with Lorenzo. No one is what he or she purports to be; all are obscured by a mask, viewed through double vision. After her father and husband murder Lorenzo and present his bones to her, the skeleton serves as a reminder of the reality beneath all their disguises.

Miramillia's own story, however, ends on a happier note. Her son returns with a woman he has saved from a villain and the girl rewards him with her hand in marriage. But this happy ending is offset by all the dolorous tales Miramillia has recounted, and *The Fruitless Enquiry* remains a sad recital of woman's woes.

The Life of Madam de Villesache

Haywood continues her investigation of women's state in *The Life of Madam de Villesache* (1727).[5] The story contains the passion and intrigue that had become Haywood's trademark, and her readers could pore over pages replete with attempted rapes, escapes, suicides, and the like; yet, as in so many of her other novels written during these years, buried within the fantastic romance is the real story that challenges the static, fictional world of innocence betrayed. In *The Life of Madam de Villesache* the horrific interior that is found under the masquerade of civilization is revealed in all its terror; the facade erected by the dominating male crumbles under the author's scathing examination of the rape of innocence.

The story begins innocently enough. Henrietta, the daughter of a duke, has been raised incognito in the country. She is a beauty and totally wins the heart of the rustic Clermont, the only son of a rich farmer. They plan a life of happiness, but her father and fate intervene, and "soon this golden Age of uncorrupted Pleasures past away" (p. 3). Her father no longer "consent[s] to bury in Obscurity, a Life which he thought deserv'd to shine with all the Illustrations the World could give it" (p. 4), and he decides to present her to the royal court. When her father learns of her attachment to Clermont, he is even more determined to remove her to the city, but not, unfortunately, before Clermont and Henrietta have consented to a secret marriage.

Their happiness is short lived, and soon Henrietta is forcibly carried to the city. Time passes; she is overwhelmed by the splendors of court life and very shortly is enmeshed in its passions and intrigues. "By degrees she began to look back on all that had past with a kind of Contempt; after which, 'tis needless to say she repented having so hastily dispos'd of herself" (p. 13). She continues to write to Clermont and "endeavor'd as much as possible in the stile of her Letter to conceal the Change there was in her Sentiments to his disadvantage" (p. 13). All too quickly, however, her "country husband" is forgotten. When a man known only as the Marquis of Ab———lle asks to marry her, Henrietta is forced to recall Clermont's existence and her first wish "never to have known a more exalted Hope, than being the wife of Clermont" (p. 17). Rather than face her father's anger at her refusal to marry the Marquis, she agrees, "falling a sacrifice to this mock marriage" (p. 21).

Henrietta does not enjoy her new "marriage" very long; from the outset "Peace . . . [is] a Stranger to her Breast" (p. 23). Thoughts of Clermont govern her waking hours, and when he appears claiming his conjugal rights, Henrietta pleads with him not to reveal her treachery, and they soon are enjoying marital privileges on the sly. Only when she and Clermont are caught by the Marquis "in a posture, which cou'd give them no room to hope an Evasion" (p. 33) do they reveal their previous marriage. Clermont is thrown into prison where he dies, it is suspected, from poison. Henrietta is sent first to a convent and then on to stand trial. This time her father helps her create a new persona for herself: "She appear'd at the Bar habited in white Sattin, as an Emblem of her Innocence" (p. 49), and she compounds the lie by pleading innocent to the charges that she knew not "what 'twas to have a tender Sentiment for any other Man" (p. 49) but her husband. She is found guilty of adultery; however, no judgment is passed about her former marriage, and her court-imposed punishment is lenient.

"Never was Indignation, Hatred, and the Desire of Revenge, arriv'd at a greater Height than in the Breast of the Marquis" (p. 55), however. Disguised as a highwayman, he brutally "stabb'd her to the Heart, with many Wounds; and as if her Death was not sufficient to satiate his rage, or still fear'd a living Heir wou'd arise from that Body to the Title of Ab——lle; he rip'd her open with an unmanly Brutality, and taking hence the Innocent unborn, stuck it on the point of his remorseless Sword, then threw it down in Scorn by the bleeding Parent" (p. 59). The Marquis is not convicted of murder, yet he is punished: he goes mad. Just before his death, in a moment of lucidity, he confesses to all his crimes.

The Life of Madam de Villesache is a tour de force for Haywood. She manages to explore, in some depth, the vacillating tempera- ments of women like Henrietta who have been raised not to use their reason. Her tragic flaw, if it may be so labeled, is, as Haywood writes, "her Indolence and Irresolution; because from them all the others [she] became guilty of, were deriv'd" (p. 55). Unable to form and adhere to her own judgments and decisions, her entire tragic life is the direct result of this vacillation. She is not morally strong enough to refuse Clermont's initial proposal or courageous enough to reject the Marquis and the life of ease he offers; nor is she able to renounce Clermont's love when he offers it a second time. At the center of Henrietta there is a certain vacuousness that Haywood carefully and explicitly reveals in conjunction with her agony of sexual exploitation, exaggerated sensibility, and female terror.

As before, this work is an examination of the male myth of women's subjugation and subservience. Clermont tries to mold and restrain Henrietta, as does the Marquis. Both attempt to force her into patterns of behavior and are so successful that she loses her entire being and exists as a mindless, directionless female. Clermont's attention finally degenerates to treating her as a sex object, a prostitute. From her initial position as an orphan to her brutal murder by the Marquis, Henrietta is given existence only by the male. He has taught her how to be deceptive, how to exist in the elaborate make-believe that is offered as a panacea to her imprisonment. The male succeeds in destroying the female through his careful articulation of her story in the myth he creates. This is Haywood's first full-length examination of persecuted innocence and its two levels of reality: male manipulation and harassment of the female and, even more, the woman's attempt to reveal, from beneath the cover of the falsehood, her own story of this rape and destruction.

Philidore and Placentia

Philidore and Placentia; or, L'Amour trop Delicat (1727)[6] is Haywood's most aggressive yet sophisticated treatment of double reality. The main plot chronicles the machinations of the aggressive Placentia, while the submerged tale is an even more flagrant story of her gross exploitation and manipulation by the controlling male society. Haywood anatomizes the manmade myth of the angelic female, revealing it for sham and exploring the process by which men create it.

Philidore falls in love with Placentia "from the first moment of seeing her" (p. 157) and quickly indulges in highly imaginative daydreams. "His fancy pictured her so divine a creature that not only himself, but all mankind beside were unworthy to be styled her servants" (p. 158). She is metamorphosized into his "angel-like Placentia" and "It was with the most enthusiastic adoration he regarded her. . . . Scarce could he think her mortal, so high an esteem had he conceived of her" (p. 158). To expose this myth-making, Haywood first reverses the usual pursuer and pursued, male/female roles twice over; then she explodes and reverses the usual romantic roles of hero and heroine and buries story within story, using her narrative technique to investigate the process.

Specifically, Philidore indulges in fabrication on two fronts, both of which lead to his destruction before he can be rescued by Haywood: not only does he create highly unrealistic visions of Placentia, as angel, goddess, and so on, but his entire initial contact with her is based on a lie. Cutting his hair, dying his complexion with walnut juice, and converting his costly apparel to homely russet robes, he transforms "the fine gentleman into a country boor" (p. 159). Haywood underscores the total absurdity of this notion that idealizes his slavish position when she writes that as Placentia's servant, "He had the boundless happiness of stealing to the coachhouse and embracing the cushions on which she sat, kissing the step on which she trod" (pp. 159–60). Her message is clear: their affair will never succeed until Philidore is able to look at Placentia realistically and behave toward her accordingly. She is neither an angel to be idolized nor a servant to be enslaved.

Placentia also begins their relationship blinded by imaginatively clouded vision. She creates an image far removed from the reality of Philidore. She allows her passion to dictate to her reason, and "She painted him in imagination the most desperate, dying love that ever was" (p. 166). He, too, possesses an "angel-like form, a behavior so elegant, a courage so undaunted, and a mien and voice so languishing and delicate" (p. 166) that clearly he is not the rustic he claims to be.

Neither character is able to deal with the reality of the other; Philidore especially cannot accept Placentia as a woman, aggressive and strong, who even has protected him from robbers; thus he withdraws so that he can indulge and feed in private the more pleasant, romantic image that he has created. This is by far Haywood's strongest indictment of the male. As she observes, "The truth is, he saw not that she loved him because he wished not she should do so. With so pure and disinterested a zeal did he worship this goddess of his soul that he desired not to inspire her with a passion which, as their circumstances were, could not but be uneasy to her" (p. 169). Philidore wants an image to idolize, a woman he can control. Placentia refuses to be cast in either role.

Predictably, when Placentia takes charge of their relationship, Philidore is shocked. Not only does she penetrate his disguise and "see the gentleman through the disguise of rusticity" (p. 173), but she begins aggressively and physically to assert herself—she attempts to seduce him:

[she] threw off all modesty, forgot all pride . . . and pitched on a desperate remedy for a desperate disease; and, having summoned all her charms into her eyes [and] passed the best part of the day in consulting what look and what habit would become her best, she put on one of the most languishing

and tender that her instructive passion could direct her to assume and,
clothing her delicate body in the richest undress, threw herself on a couch
with a studied but most engaging carelessness. Then ordering Jacobin
should attend her, [she] received him . . . catching suddenly one of his
hands and pulling him to a chair close to the couch. (pp. 174–5)

This is a key scene. Philidore will not be violated, nor will he
allow his idea of her to be desecrated; he will preserve his delusion.
He does not even attempt to kiss her, and when he exposes her
bosom in an effort to revive her after a fainting spell, Philidore
remains unaffected by her physical charms. No amount of reality
can make him change his mind and see Placentia as she truly is, a
real woman not an angel.

This scene, paradoxically enough, does not reveal the true Placentia either, for she too is disguised. Although Haywood presents
her as the ultimate in the aggressive woman, it is not the real
Placentia. Thus utterly shocked at her own behavior, she faints.
Recognizing the falseness of her disguise, Placentia is more fortunate
with the fantasy she has created, for with his hasty departure, Philidore remains the angel-man she has mentally created.

Haywood extends this device even further when she has both
characters reveal themselves through letters, that is, through more
fiction making. Again she exposes Philidore's delusion when she
has him write, "could I be brought to think of you as lovers ordinarily do of the women they adore how much beyond the reach
of words would be the happiness of my state" (p. 178). But he
remains enamored with his vision and cannot love the woman.

In an effort to preserve his illusion, Philidore leaves for Persia;
Placentia, with "most raving frenzy" (p. 180) falls into a fever, but
much to her chagrin, she recovers and withdraws to the country to
recover her reason. Meanwhile, she loses her fortune when her brother
returns to claim his share of their inheritance.

The remaining portion of the first part of the novel recounts
Philidore's adventures as he makes his way to Persia. Captured by
pirates, abandoned on an island, attacked by a tiger, Philidore
undergoes a typical hero's trials. When he rescues the Christian
Eunuch, the stage is set for another story, one more tactic Haywood
uses to denounce the fallacy of myth-making. She brilliantly underscores this increasingly important distinction between appearance
and reality and fact and fiction by means of the Eunuch's story.

The Eunuch is another example of a man deceived by his dreams and unreal creations. In a story within a story, he underscores Haywood's covert tale of female subservience to male rule. He masquerades as a painter. Unable to have the real Arithea, "Pygmalion-like, I now doted on an image of my own formation, and would kisses have inspired breath into the inanimate plate, mine must certainly have warmed it into life" (p. 201). He continues, "My time was now wholly taken up between the shadow and the substance . . . [and I found myself] no longer master of my reason" (p. 201). Like Philidore, the Eunuch has fallen in love with a dream, the illusion he has created of Arithea. When he is caught, robbed of his picture, imprisoned, "and lashed with iron whips a hundred strokes on my naked back" (p. 202) because he has looked upon Arithea, he is receiving the beating all men deserve who have used women by denying them their personal reality in the real world. Haywood is at her most aggressive. Not only is the man whipped, but when he secretly enters the seraglio where he confronts the real Arithea, he is first attacked and then castrated "by five or six armed slaves" (p. 205). With physical dismemberment comes psychological maiming, and the Eunuch no longer cares to fantasize about or dominate women.

In a final effort to eradicate the make-believe that covers reality within appropriate though pleasing images, the last portions of the novel are a careful destruction of the initial dreams and illusions. First, Philidore regains his economic power, that is, his inheritance, with the death of his uncle; next, he meets Placentia and rescues her from being sold into slavery and hears her story of her increasing independence. Placentia tells Philidore how utterly destroyed she had been by the male fiction: "Every faculty of my mind was deprived of its force, and I was in effect no more than a piece of imagery wrought by some skillful hand which walks and seems to look, yet knows not its own motions" (p. 214). This is the state to which woman has been reduced.

To elevate women's position has been Haywood's purpose in all of *Philidore and Placentia*. Exposing the myths and illusions that direct the lives of both men and women, Haywood uncovers women's double reality. She dissects man's need to create woman always in a secondary position and woman's corresponding fantasy to be the aggressor with, paradoxically, her need to create an idealized man.

Philidore and Placentia is the quintessential novel of Haywood's middle period. It reveals one of her most sophisticated attempts to study the psychology of character through intricacies of plot and the notion of image making. It also allows her to explore the nature of literature and writing and the way that they reveal the parallel reality. The adventure portion of the novel with the wanderings, rapes, shipwrecks, pirates, and so forth presents metaphoric equivalents to the turmoil and violence that are so naturally the fate of women. But the reversal in roles—Placentia's aggression, Philidore's acquiescence and submission—underscore the reality that Haywood so carefully delineates.

The Perplex'd Dutchess

The Perplex'd Dutchess; or, Treachery Rewarded (1728)[7] is as memorable as *Philidore and Placentia* thanks to its protagonist, Gigantilla, the commander of an "ambitious and aspiring Soul, and Mistress of an uncommon Share of Cunning" (p. 2). Gigantilla becomes the companion of a great lady of quality, Artemia, who is engaged to marry the wealthy Duke of Malfy, and she is soon busy taking the lady's lovers away from her, particularly the Duke. When she intrigues with him, it is "with the Air of endeavouring to conceal a Softness she was asham'd of, discover'd it in a thousand Words, and Looks, which had the appearance of the most artless Innocence, but were in reality the produce of the deepest Deceit" (p. 12). Gigantilla is playing for great stakes because she wants to be his duchess. Like Glicera of *The Fair Jilt,* Gigantilla wants to destroy female rivals and also bears a grudge against males, especially Count Philamount, who "thought her far from handsome, and was amazed to hear so many Gentlemen, infinitely her Superiors, had thought her worthy their Addresses" (p. 22). Gigantilla is the exemplar of Haywood's aggressive women, as she pits the Duke against the Count, creating a rivalry that results in the latter's death. The Duke is completely taken in by Gigantilla's treacherous lie about a liaison between Artemia and Philamount and is so "infatuated with her beauty, her dissembled Love, and well-feign'd Modesty and Virtue, that, contrary to the advice of his Council, the Entreaties of those who were most his Favourites, his own Interest and Glory," he marries Gigantilla, "and from the meanest Rank of People rais'd her to the supremest Dignity in his power to bestow" (pp. 33–4).

Gigantilla still is not satisfied; "the Fears of losing what by such indirect Means she had acquir'd empoisoned all the Felicities of her Life" (p. 34), and greedily she desires more and more power and money. She turns the Duke against his own brother, Theanor, who sees Gigantilla as she really is. Gigantilla is able to make Theanor's "most disinterested Actions appear mean, designing, and his very Virtues, Vices" (p. 36), and soon the Duke even begins to doubt his brother's sagacity and integrity.

"But now the time approach'd which was ordain'd to show this haughty Woman there was a Power Supreme, which, when it pleas'd cou'd put a stop to the further Progress of her pernicious Designs" (p. 53). While she is en route to Sicily with the Duke, he suddenly dies. Her intrigue with Nearchus, a courtier to whom she had promised love if he would help her with her base designs, is discovered by the now-ruling Theanor, and at the end Gigantilla is exiled and powerless. "All her Artifices, all her Policy now fail'd her, she was [as] incapable of doing Service to herself, or hurt to others, as an Ideot" (p. 59).

As in *The Life of Madam de Villesache*, Haywood again creates the "worst of women." Although Gigantilla is politically punished at the end (there is no mention of moral retribution), and the good characters survive and go on to rule, *The Perplex'd Dutchess* is important not because of its obvious moral, but because of its not so subliminal tale of anger and hatred. Gigantilla is the most forceful of Haywood's surrogate selves. In an effort to lash out at the all-controlling male, the author creates a woman who controls, corrupts, and destroys one of the most important men of the age. This is a woman's story, an unvarnished tale of power over the male. Only at the end, with Theanor's rise to rule, does Haywood return to the comforting story that sees vice punished and virtue rewarded, and that witnesses woman put in her proper subservient place.

The Padlock, Irish Artifice, and *Persecuted Virtue*

Haywood continues to write on this theme in several other novels of this middle period. *The Padlock; or, No Guard Without Virtue* (1728), *Irish Artifice; or, The History of Clarina* (1728), and *Persecuted Virtue; or, The Cruel Lover* (1728) reiterate the tale of man's rescue and dominance of a violated and fettered female. The story has been delineated earlier; there is not much that is new in the presentation.

The author clearly hopes that the sheer number of her novels will convince her readers of the woman's plight as much as the stories themselves.

The Padlock,[8] for example, tells of the youthful Violante, who is forced by her parents to marry the aging Don Lepido because they want the money the union will bring; it is an extraordinarily frightening description of a woman's total imprisonment in marriage. Because of male dominance, love is transformed into hate, and "it was only by Compulsion he enjoyed her as his Wife" (p. 59); she is repeatedly and legally raped by "this Tyrant of her Tranquility" (p. 60). Violante is physically violated by her husband and mentally by her parents through their desire to marry her off for financial gain. But such tortures are not enough; "Never was a Prisoner under Sentence confin'd with greater Strictness; [her husband] debarr'd her the Society of her nearest Relations, Women as well as Men, permitted not even her Father Confessor to be alone with her, let her have no Male Servants . . . and he oblig'd her to wear one of those Machines, which in other countries are so much ridicul'd" (p. 58), a chastity belt. Violante becomes a symbol of why Haywood is writing and what she wants to guard her readers against becoming.

Irish Artifice[9] tells of the persecution of Clarina. She is so harassed and tormented by Merovious and his mother, Aglaura, that she does not have enough strength to counter their attacks. She is transformed from innocent maid into insipid prostitute.

Persecuted Virtue[10] is perhaps the best example of the novels after *Cleomelia, Philidore and Placentia,* and *The Perplex'd Duchess* in its dramatization of the destruction of the female. Serinda is initially in love with Hersilius when she loses her fortune. She loses her suitors as well, and is forced to marry Clodio, her only remaining beau. Serinda is faithful to him, though she continues to love Hersilius, whom she frees from debtor's prison by paying his debts. She refuses to see Hersilius again, however, and thus obeys "the rigid dictates of her Virtue" (p. 16).

But Serinda's future is not to be so placid. Theander, a friend of her husband's, falls in love with her. When she refuses his advances, he tries to rape her, but she escapes by jumping out of a window. To get even, Theander plots her ruin. He tells Clodio about Serinda's continued relationship with Hersilius. The former lovers have met only publicly in order to keep their relationship innocent, but twisted by Theander, it appears sordid and adulterous. Clodio, of course, is shocked. He changes his will, then abruptly dies. Theander becomes executor of the will and forces Serinda to leave home. She has been diminished almost to nothingness, "reduced from Grandeur to the want of even the most common Necessaries of Life, denied the Privilege of seeing her own Child . . . [and] without the Friends to comfort, advise, or relieve her under these Calamities" (p. 52). The story ends with Serinda exiled to Geneva and Hersilius banished.

The Agreeable Caledonian and *The Fair Hebrew*

In the final analysis, *Persecuted Virtue* remains a stridently explicit story of female subjugation and persecution; however, it does not reach the wrathful heights of *The Perplex'd Duchess*. Perhaps Haywood was led to create Clementina, her aggressive spokeswoman in *The Agreeable Caledonian; or, Memoirs of Signiora di Morella* (1728),[11] out of a desire to make up for the suffering silence of Serinda.

The story begins with Clementina, who "was of a Disposition which made her impatient of Controul, and violently addicted to follow her own Will" (p. 20), pursued by the Cardinal, but she is untouched by his passion. Rumors arise from their association, and Clementina is labeled a prostitute. To save her name and reputation, her father sends Clementina to the Augustine convent at Viterbo, which is very similar to a prison. Failure to obey her father's and her suitor's wishes results in premature death.

At the convent, Clementina meets the lovesick Signiora Miramene and learns of her passion for Baron Glencairn. At first Clementina offers to help the lovers, but meeting Glencairn herself, she quickly reverses her friendship and becomes Miramene's enemy by trying to gain Glencairn for herself. After much plotting, many fabrications, and several attempts, Clementina escapes from the convent with Glencairn and "thus enter'd into the fatal Labyrinth" (p. 85).

Labyrinths are important in Haywood's works. She employs her usual device of the tale within the tale and first has Miramene relate her story; then, buried within that account is the first-person narrative of Signiora Jacinta del Tortosa, another of Glencairn's mistresses. Both women tell of overwhelming love for men not their husbands. Jacinta's history, at the very center of the narrative, reveals the most intimate oppression and exploitation to which women are subject. This layering of the interpolated tale with which she "imprisons" her overt story mirrors the fettering to which women are

subject. Women hide and are enchained (perhaps actions differing
but in degree) because the reality of their lives cannot be overtly
presented.

Jacinta's husband not only tortures her, but declares he is Miramene's lover as well. He is a lover who does not love but punishes;
he attacks Miramene, who "rav'd . . . tore the Villain's face and
Garments, and, in spight of his Efforts to stop my Mouth, sent
forth a Cry" (p. 50). To emphasize males' imprisoning of females
further, Haywood has Jacinta and Miramene share Glencairn (although by this time he has almost completely rejected Jacinta). If,
the tale seems to imply, even a few men can sexually captivate and
manipulate women, the true story of the female condition will never
be untangled and heard.

The interweaving of plot and characters underscores the entanglement that is women's lot: they are trapped in falsehood and
adultery in their lives, and in their loves. There is no conclusion
to the piece. Clementina and Glencairn lead a dissolute life together
in Paris where she contracts a fever and dies. He is unpunished and
unregenerate at the end.

In *The Fair Hebrew; or, A True, but Secret History of Two Jewish
Ladies* (1729),[12] Haywood tries once again to create an aggressive
woman. Kesiah is a woman who knows her own mind from the
first. When Dorante is first attracted to her, Kesiah makes her
position very clear: she will have nothing less than marriage. Unfortunately, neither of their fathers recognizes the union, and Dorante is cut off from his inheritance. Without money, Kesiah scorns
him and decamps with his gold (what is left of it) and a new gallant.
Dorante is comforted by a younger brother and then dies of grief
when he learns that Kesiah and her paramour have been taken
prisoner and carried to Madagascar "to continue in a hard and
perpetual slavery" (p. 52). In the final analysis, *The Fair Hebrew*
remains flat, the characters undeveloped.

The Adventures of Eovaai

Haywood returns in 1736 to the roman à clef and the popularity
she had achieved with *The Court of Carimania* and *Memoirs of a Certain
Island Adjacent to the Kingdom of Utopia.*

The Adventures of Eovaai, Princess of Ijaveo[13] begins in a never-never
land of pre-Edenic splendor, as Haywood writes in her dedicatory

letter, a time when "the World [was] before Adam"; the Kingdom of Ijaveo is peace itself. The Edenlike atmosphere is soon shattered, however, as the selfish desires of man for money and power erupt. After seven years of peaceful reign, the trouble begins when Eovaai, the Princess of Ijaveo, loses a precious jewel, a carcenet, that had been given to her by her father. Dreadful gloom, sulfurous fires, secret plots, and open rebellion are the result of this loss, and "Ijaveo became the scene of Civil War" (p. 16). Eovaai is abandoned by all her rational counselors and advisors, and only the wicked Ochihatou, prime minister of the neighboring Hypotosa, remains.[14] (He has studied black magic and has not only caused the death of Hypotosa's king through his magical arts, but has had the young prince, Adelhu, banished and is busy promoting his own ambition and lusts.) At first, he is unable to influence Eovaai, for she is very strong willed; however, repeated assaults on her reason soon succeed, and Ochihatou wheedles his way into Eovaai's affection. "The Precepts she received were yet green, there wanted Age to confirm and spread their roots, so as to enable her to bring forth the Fruit expected from her" (pp. 6–7). Her naivete is just what Ochihatou needs, and soon he has all but converted her to his evil way of thinking. She is transformed from the sweet, caring, innocent, and reasonable female into a vain flirt. She "despised the Sessions of her Youth; looked on it as a Meanness of Spirit to study for the Good of Inferiors; and considering subjects as Slaves thought it the just Prerogative of the Monarch to dispose at pleasure [of] all their lives and Properties" (p. 41). She has forgotten all the teaching of her father; she has destroyed the idyllic peace that existed in her realm. Eovaai has subtly been transformed from the docile, acquiescent woman who is approved of by everyone, to the expression of Haywood's insidious anger and frustration.

As the story continues, Eovaai is saved by the Genii Halafamai, who reveals Ochihatou in his true colors—"crooked, deformed, distorted in every limb and Feature . . . encompassed with a thousand hideous Forms, which sat upon his Shoulders, clung round his Hands . . . to dictate all his Words and Gestures" (p. 78). Eovaai escapes from him by substituting one of Ochihatou's former mistresses in her own place. (This lady had the misfortune to be in a monkey's body, but Eovaai turns her back into female form.) Ochihatou apprehends Eovaai yet again and is on the point of raping her, but Eovaai fights back, "resolved to hazard every thing . . . rather than consent to sacrifice her Chastity to the Enchanter's Will"

(p. 193). She breaks his wand, the source of his evil power. Just
then a young stranger comes to her rescue and in anger and frustration at the disruption of his plans, Ochihatou dashes his own
brains out against an oak tree. Her hero turns out to be none other
than the banished prince, Adelhu. They are wed, the lost jewel is
found, and both the prince and the princess live long, happy lives.
Similar to *Philidore and Placentia, The Adventures of Eovaai* recreates
in splendid, magical moments the final championing of rational
control over irrational forces. More important, it reveals Haywood's
continued interest in chastizing her women readers for suppressing
their aggressive natures.

Haywood's purpose throughout her popular novels has been to
reveal her feelings. She created Gigantillas, Henriettas, Clementi-
nas, and Gliceras in an effort to reveal the anger and aggression that
lie within women, herself most especially. *The Adventures of Eovaai*
reinvokes and heightens the aggressive qualities she had portrayed
in the majority of her early novels. Like Ochihatou's evil "ypre"
that "twisted its envenom'd Tail round the Heart of Eovaai, and,
in an instant, erased all the maxims the wise Ijaveo had endeavored
to establish there" (p. 41), so Haywood would dominate the mind
of her reader. Giving free rein to all libertinism and immoral passions, Eovaai becomes Haywood's strongest criticism of the position
of women in society. By displaying the total licentiousness to which
women can descend if they are continually bound, Haywood reveals
the harm that is being done to them. Since this is surely one of the
most rage-filled of Haywood's novels, it is well that it is disguised
in a fairy-tale aura, for what it reveals about the female condition
is truly shocking.

Summary

The popular novel of the early years of the eighteenth century
celebrated order: reason triumphed over passion, virtue won over
evil, and the good lived happily ever after. Most frequently in
romances by contemporary novelists, the heroine was tested and
tried by the scheming, conniving villain, but she remained true to
herself, her principles, and her virtue, and was rewarded with a
marriage to the hero at the conclusion. This myth can be translated
as the triumphing of the rational powers over the irrational that
challenge but do not overcome. Marriage celebrates the union of

reason with feeling, sense with sensibility. The virtuous heroine is perhaps temporarily blinded by passion, like Placentia, but ultimately, passion is controlled by reason, and the heroine by the hero.

Far from championing domestic and social order, during her early years Haywood was challenging such accepted solutions. If her novels did end with a marriage, it was a union achieved only after severe trials and tests had been endured. Haywood seemed to be unable to close her eyes to the irrational side of human nature, and rather than consistently and constantly forcing a contrived conclusion on her readers, she felt justified in depicting the world as she saw it.

That world was bleak indeed. Women were shunted aside, heroines were tormented and harassed. Not until her novels of the 1740s and the 1750s did Haywood readjust her vision and begin to see marriage as a peaceable solution to the war between the sexes.

Chapter Eight
The Later Novels, 1741–1756

The Adventures of Eovaai, published in 1736 (reprinted in 1741 as *The Unfortunate Princess; or, The Ambitious Statesman),* was the last of Haywood's productions for almost ten years. This silence was nothing the author had planned for herself, but it was necessary after she was defamed by Alexander Pope in *The Dunciad.* Pope had originally intended his work as a piece of vitriolic satire damaging to the multitude of scurrilous hack writers of the period.[1] Unfortunately, because of her attack on Henrietta Howard in *The Secret History of the Present Intrigues of the Court of Carimania,* Eliza Haywood was included.

In addition, Pope felt justified in his assault on Haywood because she was the friend of William Bond, Daniel Defoe, and Aaron Hill, all shameless scribblers in Pope's estimation. He also thought Haywood was responsible for a personal attack on him[2] in *The Court of Lilliput,* a work no longer attributed to her because the style is unlike that of her known works and because the narrator indulges in far too many sarcasms made at the expense of women to acknowledge Haywood's hand in the production. Whatever Pope's motive, the passage in *the Dunciad* included some of the most vulgar lines in poem (the original version was even more brutal; see pt.2 ll. 137–48, 170; pt.3, ll. 149–53). Eliza, "yon Juno of majestic size / With cow-like udders, and with ox-like eyes" (2, ll. 163–4), is offered as the chief prize in the bookseller's games. "Osborne and Curll accept the glorious strife. . . . One on his manly confidence relies, / One on his vigour and superior size" (2, ll. 167–70). Curll, of course, wins the contest, but loses the war. His sexual prowess is depleted when the Goddess of Dulness finishes with him. This work would seem to be directed mainly against booksellers, but it is quite clear that Pope had no use for female writers either, and, as the most popular and prolific of the lot, Haywood was the chief object of his ridicule.

Haywood herself made no attempt to answer Pope, but the infamous Curll concocted *The Female Dunciad,* in which he included Haywood's *Irish Artifice; or, The History of Clarina* (1728). The novel itself is innocuous enough, but Haywood was castigated by Richard Savage for her quick return to the literary fray. In his *An Author to be Let* (1732), he writes:

When Mrs. Haywood ceas'd to be a Strolling Actress, why might not the Lady (tho' once a Theatrical Queen) have subsisted by turning Washerwoman? Has not the Fall of Greatness been a frequent Distress in all Ages? She might have caught a beautiful Bubble as it arose from the Suds of her Tub, blown it in Air, seen it glitter, and then break! Even in this low Condition, she had play'd with a Bubble, and what more is the Vanity of human Greatness? She might also have consider'd the sullied Linnen growing white in her pretty red Hands, as an Emblem of her Soul, were it well scoured by Repentance for the Sins of her Youth: but she rather chooses starving by writing Novels of Intrigue, to teach young Heiresses the Art of running away with Fortune-hunters, and scandalizing Persons of the highest Worth and Distinction.[3]

These attacks did not stop Haywood, although she was silenced temporarily; when she did return to novel writing, her works were published anonymously. Before being excoriated by Pope, she had been an author of extreme popularity. Her name sold books.[4] After *The Dunciad* affair, her name no longer appeared on the title page, but her novels remained as popular and powerful as ever.

Although the decade from 1731 to 1741 saw her producing fewer novels than during any single year of her earlier period, she did continue to write. Her translation of de Mouhy's *La Paysanne Parvenue* as *The Virtuous Villager; or, Virgin's Victory* (1742) helped her to reestablish contact with the reading public and allowed her a chance to try her hand at the new domestic novel that had been important on the literary scene since the extraordinary success of *Pamela* in 1740. As advertised in *The Virtuous Villager,* Haywood's career took another turn at this time when she tried her hand at publishing. Her list of published works is not extensive: *The Busy-Body; or, Successful Spy,* a translation of de Mouhy's best-known *La Mouche, ou les aventures et espièglieries facétieuses de Bigand* (1736), and *Anti-Pamela; or, Feign'd Innocence detected, in a Series of Syrena's Adventures;* these were the only volumes to come out of her shop at the "sign of Fame in Covent Garden."

Anti-Pamela

After her forced silence, Haywood returned to the literary scene with *Anti-Pamela; or, Feign'd Innocence Detected* (1741)[5]; it was her last attempt to produce a sensually stimulating novel. Written at the beginning of her "new" period, *Anti-Pamela* is a reversion to her earlier type of story. Syrena is a prostitute, and the book records her peripatetic career.

Syrena began her occupation early in life; "She had not reach'd her thirteenth year, before she excell'd the most experienc'd Actress on the stage, in a lively assuming [of] all the different Passions that find Entrance in a Female Mind" (p. 2). She creates characters and adjusts her deportment to suit them; "her colour would come and go, her Eyes sparkle, grow Languid, or overflow with Tears, her Bosom heave, her Limbs tremble; she would fall into Faintings, or appear transported, and as it were out of herself" (p. 3). Syrena becomes very proficient at this art of appearing other than she really is. But this is deceptive make-believe, harmful to a woman's well being. In *Anti-Pamela,* such falsity is used only to trap rich lovers and obtain wealth for Syrena, and does not lead to good female mental health. Fantasies provide temporary, material relief, but not long-term gain. Haywood exposes this deception through Syrena's life.

Syrena first entices Lieutenant Vardine and soon has him supplying her with money. She continues to fabricate tales and extract money from him until, one day, Vardine fails to appear at their assignation. He writes to say that his regiment has been called up, but the inference is that he does not care to pay her any more visits, nor will he believe any more of her stories. "But she was capable of loving in reality nothing but herself, and carried on a Correspondence with him merely on a mercenary View, she was not much to be pitied" (p. 46).

Next, she gets a position reading to an elderly lady of quality who has a handsome husband and a twenty-two-year-old son, both of whom are soon attracted to Syrena. The son kidnaps Syrena, pledging undying love for her and calls her "his Life, his Soul, Cherubim—Goddess" (p. 81). She counterfeits a faint and falls "dying on the floor" (p. 82) to avoid the inevitable rape. Since the son is penniless she sets her sights on the father. Her choice is based upon her ability to control and, like Haywood, she does so by making up stories.[6] But all still leads to the same end: lover after lover initally is taken in by her schemes and fabrications, but soon discovers the falseness of tale and teller and abandons her. Syrena Tricksy remains untouched, for "the Wretch [was] incapable of either . . . Penitence or Remorse" (p. 107).

We watch her become the coquette with Mr. D. and exchange her person for his gold; she meets Lord R. and sleeps with him; then she seduces a mercer; she pretends to sprain her ankle and attracts a young gallant; finally, she contracts a venereal disease. Syrena is unabashed, but her mother, who "first taught her to ensnare, to deceive, and to betray [aimed only] to enable her by those Arts to secure to herself some one Man, by whom she might make her Fortune; [she] never imagined she would . . . run such length, meerly . . . to gratify Desires, which once indulg'd, bring on inevitable Destruction" (p. 178).

Her mother's fears prove to be true as Syrena's affairs multiply. Mr. W. and another gallant, who is W.'s own son, share her favors. When these affairs are exposed, she attaches herself to Mr. P., who also leaves her. Syrena feels exploited; "the Notion she had been bred up in, that a Woman who had Beauty to attract the Men, and cunning to manage them afterwards, was secure in making her Fortune, appeared now altogether fallaciousness; since she had not been able to do it in four Years incessant Application" (p. 261). She is finally undone by her last lover's wife. Mrs. E. makes up her own stories to expose Syrena; she succeeds, and Syrena is exiled to Wales.

Syrena is the most blatant victim of male exploitation and self-aggrandizement in Haywood's works. She has prostituted herself to man's notion of woman. She has totally lost any concept of self. She is fatally enslaved.

The Fortunate Foundlings

Haywood's later career as a conservative novelist really got under way in 1744 with *The Fortunate Foundlings*.[7] With the introduction of Richardson's new "kitchen morality,"[8] moral instruction, good works, and the triumph of extraordinary good over incredible evil became the dominant tone of all literary productions. Charity and generosity were the guidelines of the day, and were manifested by the foundling hospital, which became the subject of several literary

works: the anonymous *Foundling Hospital for Wit and Humor* (1743),
Moore's comedy *The Foundling* (1748), and Fielding's *The History of
Tom Jones, A Foundling* (1749).

Haywood's contribution to this fad to "encourage Virtue in both
Sexes" (Preface, *The Fortunate Foundlings*) was a rather cut and dried
tale of the history of Louisa and Horatio, twin brother and sister,
who, abandoned as infants, are brought up by the benevolent Dorilaus. Louisa is truly one of Pamela's daughters; reared as a model
of virtue, she finds she must flee the house to escape what she thinks
are her guardian's "advances," which are, in reality, only solicitous
gestures. Since she cannot return his affections in the way she imagines he wants them returned, she leaves and finds a position as a
milliner's apprentice, whose house is "a kind of rendezvous where
all the young and gay of both sexes daily resorted" (p. 24). Haywood
continues, "The adventures she was witness of made her, indeed,
more knowing of the world, but were far from corrupting those
excellent morals she had received from nature" (p. 25). Her beauty
provides temptations, not protection, and soon she has to dodge
unwanted attentions. To escape these, she goes to Windsor, where
she meets Melanthe and becomes her companion on a continental
tour. No matter how opulent or lavish her surroundings or her
suitors, Louisa "retain'd the same sincerity of mind, love of virtue,
and detestation of vice, she brought with her from the house of
Dorilaus" (p. 42). Being priggish, she is highly censorious of Melanthe's intrigue with Bellfleur. But when Melanthe discovers what
she thinks is an affair between Louisa and Bellfleur, she banishes
Louisa to England.

Poor, unsuspecting Louisa is besieged even there; Bellfleur follows
her and attempts to rape her. Fortunately she is saved by Du Plessis,
a true gallant, who falls immediately in love with her. She refuses
him. He "represented to her in the most pathetic terms, that her
innocence could have no sure protection but in the arms of a husband,
or the walls of a convent: and on his knees beseeched her, for the
sake of that virtue which she so justly prized, since she would not
accept of him for the one, to permit him to place her in that other
only asylum for a person in her circumstances" (p. 168).

Du Plessis is unaware how very apt his observation is, for this is
the entire focus of Louisa's portion of *The Fortunate Foundlings*—this
emphasis on the battle between imprisonment in marriage or in a
convent. Either one, if done for the wrong reasons, is tantamount

to eternal enslavement either to a tyrannical husband or self-righteous god. This is, as Haywood noted, the feminine dilemma; however, in *The Fortunate Foundlings* she is unable to present the struggle with the great immediacy that is evident in her other works. Louisa does ultimately marry Du Plessis, but she remains a cardboard figure who does not invite reader's interest. She is a bit too pontificating, a little too sanctimonious to inspire attention and involvement. Louisa does not fantasize; all situations are perceived with the eyes of truth, and there is no need covertly to present a vision that differs from the reality. Like Haywood's fictional technique, she remains distant and cold.

Horatio also suffers from being presented too rigidly, almost sanctimoniously. He joins the service as a volunteer in Flanders, is taken captive by the French, is freed by the Chevalier, and becomes enamoured of the beautiful Charlotta de Palfoy, one of the ladies attending Princess Louisa Maria Theresa. To win her affections, he joins the Swedish campaign. Charlotta, another of Haywood's beleaguered innocents, in the meantime has fended off de Coigney, one of her most pressing suitors, and eagerly awaits Horatio's return. Horatio is taken prisoner by the Russians but finally is set free and is able to marry her.

By recounting the deeds and adventures of Louisa, Horatio, and Charlotta, Haywood is able to give examples of both male and female virtue. Gone are the racy details of escapades of the earlier tales; in their stead, we meet the sober hero and heroine of the author's new rational mode. Sensational material has given way to moralistic reporting, and Haywood is at pains, both in this and her next novel, to underscore that she is dealing with real, not fictitious, characters who can therefore be considered as good, moral, object lessons. She attempts little in the way of under-cover plot and seems comfortable just telling her moral tale.

Life's Progress through the Passions

Haywood's moral seriousness is even more evident in her next novel, *Life's Progress through the Passions: or, the Adventures of Natura* (1748).[9] Emphasizing this tone, she writes in the Introduction:

I am an enemy to all *romances, novels,* and whatever carries the air of them
. . . and as it is a *real,* not *fictitious* character I am about to present, I
think myself obliged . . . to draw him such as he was, not such as some

sanguine imaginations might wish him to have been. I flatter myself, however, that *truth* will appear not altogether void of charms, and the adventures I take upon me to relate, not be less pleasing for being within the reach of probability, and such as might have happened to any other as well as the person they did. (pp. 2–3)

Haywood is now concerned with the ordinariness of life, and rather than an ultragood or ultrabad character, for "There never yet was any one man, in whom all the *Virtues,* or all the *Vices,* were summed up" (p. 2), she creates Natura, her everyman. "Few there are, I am pretty certain, who will not find some resemblance of himself in one part or other of his life . . . [and will] also be reminded in what manner the passions operate in every stage of life, and how far the constitution of the *outward frame* is concerned in the emotions of the *internal faculties*" (p. 3). The characters are drawn with less brilliance and sparkle than those in her earlier works. She is still concerned with portraying inward agitations through the disguise of outward calm, and to a lesser degree the principal tale masks a rebellious, turbulent story.

The story begins with Natura's birth to well-to-do but not op- ulently rich parents. His mother's sudden death and his father's hasty remarriage, Natura's attack of smallpox, his education at Eton, and his boyish love for Delia are events quickly described and passed over in the early pages. Haywood is less concerned with actual events than with tracing the psychological influences of the wicked step- mother, the indulgent old nurse, and indolent father on Natura's developing self-conception and intellect.

Because of his inexperience of the world, most especially of women, he soon becomes entangled with Harriet, a well-endowed courtesan, who deftly manages their torrid but short-lived affair; her lawyer draws up "double contracts" and they become "man and wife" on paper. Harriet demands a large sum of money that is impossible for him to raise. When his father learns of the extortion, he locks Natura into his room; on the third day the young man escapes and goes directly to Harriet only to find her in the arms of another man. Natura is shocked and turns to gambling rooms and bordellos to vent his frustration and anger.

In an effort to save his son, Natura's father arranges a European tour, and Natura and his tutor are packed up and sent on their way. Unfortunately, the tutor dies in Paris, and Natura is "left to himself, and at liberty to pursue whatever he had a fancy for" (p. 63). And so begins a combination travelog and catalog of Natura's adventures. He goes from love affair to love affair, almost marrying four women and finally marrying "a young, beautiful lady of his father's recommendation" (p. 155) Her untimely death drives him to a second marriage with the niece of a statesman, who teaches him the misery of having a luxurious, demanding, and unfaithful wife. Their marriage becomes "indeed a kind of farce acted by this unhappy pair, in which both played their parts so awkwardly, that the real character would frequently peep out, and though each dissembled, yet neither was deceived" (p. 165). Natura gets a divorce after he finds his wife in bed with his brother.

In the meantime, Natura's father and his son by his beloved first wife have died; Natura knows absolute despair. In an effort to clear his mind of his grief, he joins the French service, and there, in a romantic background, meets a young widow. *"Natura* adored *Charlotte,* not because she was a lovely woman, but because he imagined somewhat *{sic}* angelic in her mind; and *Charlotte* loved *Natura,* not because he was an agreeable person, but because she thought she discovered more charms in his soul, than in that of any other man or woman" (p. 209). They marry and have three sons. There is certainly a new tone to this romance and a sobriety not present in the conclusions of earlier novels. There are no flamboyant characters, no disastrous ending; the story carefully balances Natura's initial romantic fantasies with the sober condition of growing up and growing old. Haywood's view is one of solemnity and reason.

Although Natura's adventures, when told in such a cursory manner, do not seem very different from those that occupied the heroines of her earlier works, one must notice that Haywood's focus in *Life's Progress* is more on the moral than on the story. She writes toward the end of the novel "Man is a stranger to nothing, more than to himself;—the recesses of his own heart, are no less impenetrable to him, than the worlds beyond the moon;—he is blinded by vanity, and agitated by desires he knows not he is possessed of" (p. 206). She tries to clarify these gray, unexplored, unknown areas, but less successful than in earlier attempts, she examines them here only prosaically. In the earlier novels, the fictions themselves explored these unknown areas; here, unable to allow the tales to talk for themselves, Haywood pontificates.

Dalinda

Dalinda; or, The Double Marriage (1749)[10] was originally thought
to have been written by someone else. Its style, use of letters, and
certain turns of expression, however, almost conclusively point to
Haywood's authorship.[11] Like *Life's Progress through the Passions, Dalinda*
is concerned with portraying ordinary life in an instructive
manner. As Haywood writes in the Preface, "The Reader must
therefore expect no perfect Character.—I have drawn my Heroes
and Heroine, such as they really are, without any Illustration, either
of their Virtues, or their Defects.—Here are no poetical Descriptions,
no Flights of Imagination, I have put no Rapsodies into their
Mouths, and if I have not made them speak just as they did, I have
at least made them speak as Persons in their Circumstances would
naturally do" (pp. vi–vii). Haywood's "sole Design . . . is to shew
both Sexes, the Danger of inadvertently giving way to the Passions
of what kind soever—all lead us into Error—all have a Tendency
to Vice" (p. ix). Truth alone, she assures the reader, has been her
guide.

Dalinda was raised in the country but now resides in London.
Naive and unsophisticated, she falls in love with her obnoxious
cousin, Malvolio, and agrees to marry him. Malvolio deludes her
with an unregistered marriage and has no scruples about simultaneously
truly marrying the wealthy Flavilla. He wants to have both
women and tries to bargain with Dalinda, but she indignantly retorts
that she is not "now the easy suffering Fool I have been" (p. 85).
She returns to her grandmother's house, where she alerts her brother
and her still faithful lover, Leander, to the actions of her perfidious
"husband," for she now knows her marriage is a sham. The last half
of the novel becomes complicated with lawyers, letters, and lawsuits
as Dalinda pursues her revenge on Malvolio; she considers him "a
man who only aim'd at keeping her the Slave of his loose Desires,
to live with her [as a] Prostitute . . . and at last abandon her to
bewail alone her Infamy" (pp. 184–85). Dalinda has been emotionally
crippled; she cannot return to Leander, nor is she able to
receive any compensation from Malvolio. The story ends in a stalemate
with all parties unhappy. "Thus is [Leander] of the most
generous of Mankind rendered one of the most miserable, by a
hopeless, yet ever-during Passion.— Thus is *Dalinda* become the
most forlorn, abandoned, and disconsolate of her sex, by having

unhappily given way to the Dictates of an inconsiderable Flame;—
and thus is Malvolio, by scrupling nothing for the Gratitude of his
Wishes, deprived of his every Wish" (p. 287).

The book provides a moral lesson for all, but as in *Life's Progress,*
its lesson is more bluntly presented than in the earlier novels. An
element of a public preachiness prevents the book from being thought
of as highly as others of Haywood's works. There is little attempt
to do more than write the tale of female exploitation, and *Dalinda*
appears to be a mere repetition of earlier themes without the sophisticated strategy of double writing that Haywood had so effectively employed before.

A Letter from H—— G——g, Esq.

Haywood's next work, *A Letter from H—— G——g, Esq., One
of the Gentlemen of the Bedchamber of the Young Chevalier* (1750), [12] is
an oddly inflated pastiche of her old romance strain coupled with
her new moral tone. The journey motif allows the Prince to expound
his political views while talking to various noblemen he encounters
along his way. The Prince also becomes the romantic hero as he
rescues a young woman from a fire; in true hero fashion, he does
not take advantage of her and is therefore a model of morality and
correct behavior. The last part of this small work becomes a political
potpourri of allusions to contemporary scandals, intrigues, and the
like. *A Letter from H—— G——g, Esq.* is interesting from a literary
point of view because it exhibits the clash of romance with moral
instruction. It does not succeed because of Haywood's inability to
reconcile the divergent themes.

The History of Cornelia

Another work now attributed to Haywood, but first thought to
be written by someone else, is the 1750 *History of Cornelia,* [13] an
example, if one believes the "Advertisement," of "sentiment [which]
may, if not instruct in the knowledge, yet animate in the practice
of virtue" and of the moral and righteous behavior so much in vogue
in the late 1740s and 1750s.

The story is typical. Upon the death of her father, Cornelia goes
to live with her uncle Octavio; his son, another Octavio, falls in
love with her, but Cornelia runs away. She is helped in her escape
by Bernardo, who soon declares his own love for her. They too,

part, and Cornelia makes her way to Paris, where first she boards
in a house of prostitution and then quickly moves to the home of
a milliner. "Entirely ignorant of all the customs of the world,
unknown to all in it . . . . exposed to all the distresses" (pp. 26–
7), Cornelia finds that life on her own is complicated and filled
with dangers. She is proposed to by almost every man she meets
and is even abducted by one of her suitors, Monsieur De Rhee. She
flees from him, is recaptured, escapes, and so on, with almost
monotonous regularity. Although obviously portraying the condition of women, the plot is fatuous. As in *Dalinda,* Haywood does
not take any pains with a deeper message and instead, lets the
surface tale of persecuted innocence carry the entire story. One is
relieved at the end when Cornelia finally marries Bernardo, for only
then does her senseless, meaningless persecution stop. There is thus
a certain dullness in *The History of Cornelia* that makes the theme
of virtue in distress even more dismal, more frightening than its
presentation in her earlier novels. The very mundaneness of the
telling makes the implication most terrifying. There would appear
to be no relief from the persecution; only male tyranny and dominance determine when it is to end and when she is allowed to marry
Bernardo. Haywood returns in her next novel to a more subtly and
psychologically crafted version of her perennial subject matter.

The History of Miss Betsy Thoughtless

Haywood reached "the full fruition of her powers as a novelist,"[14]
Whicher remarks, in her next two novels, *The History of Miss Betsy
Thoughtless* (1751)[15] and *The History of Jemmy and Jenny Jessamy* (1753).
Betsy Thoughtless is a "humor" character whose chief characteristic
is denoted by her name. "Though not fundamentally vicious," Whicher
continues, "her heedless vanity, inquisitiveness, and vivacity lead
her into all sorts of follies and embarrassments upon her first entry
into fashionable life in London."[16] Betsy is a typical eighteenth-
century heroine in the first half of the novel, which traces her flights
of fancy, feelings, and sensibilities; the second half is a sober picture
of her development toward and acceptance of reason as the way of
life.

The novel owes much to Haywood's brief theatrical experiences.
The characters' names and qualities represent stock figures of Restoration drama. Besides the heroine, we find Mr. Trueworth, the

hero, whose value and goodness are unerring throughout the novel. Similarly, Mr. Munden (mundane) in his ordinariness is one of the temptations Betsy must overcome. Minor characters, too, are reminiscent of the stage, for example, Miss Nancy Forward, the prostitute; Master Sparkish, a suitor; and Mr. Goodman, a guardian.

Betsy's growth from flirt to reasonable woman is allegorical, and the novel is a bildungsroman in its concern for the progress of a young woman. Not only Betsy but the reader, Haywood notes, "will see into the secret springs which set this fair machine in motion." (1, p. 11), will learn, in other words, to perceive one's positon correctly. The "secret springs," as in her earlier fiction, will be found in hidden meanings.

After her father's death, Betsy is left in the care of Mr. Goodman, a wealthy merchant, and Mr. Trusty, a neighbor. She exhibits hoydenish qualities that bring about her temporary downfall: "hurried by an excess of vanity and that love of pleasure so natural to youth, she indulged herself in liberties of which she foresaw not the consequence. . . . [And] as a ship without ballast is tossed about at the Pleasure of every wind that blows, so was she hurried through the ocean of life, just as each predominant passion directed" (1, p. 57).

Patterning her behavior on that of Lady Mellasin, Goodman's wife, Betsy quickly learns the sources and uses of feminine power. When her first beau, the son of an alderman, appears, Betsy "used him ill and well by turns, taking an equal pleasure in raising, or depressing, his hopes, and, in spite of her good nature, felt no satisfaction superior to that of the consciousness of power of giving pain to the man who loved her." (1, p. 22).

Her behavior is reckless and thoughtless. Going to Oxford to visit her brother Francis, she is almost raped by another Oxonian, who is led on and baited by her seemingly devil-may-care attitude. She is only saved by the unexpected entrance of her brother. The repercussions of this act on Betsy and her self-image are worse than the wounds her brother receives in the ensuing duel. Betsy and Miss Flora, her companion in this escapade, are shunned by polite society and find the rumors spreading about them to be so oppressive that the women are forced to return to London.

Betsy still has not learned her lesson. Introduced to two other young men, Mr. Staple and Mr. Trueworth, she continues her coquettish airs: "All the ideas she had of either of them, served only to excite in her the pleasing imagination, how, when they both came to address her, she should play the one against the other, and give herself a constant round of diversion by their alternate contentment or disquiet" (1, p. 143).

Unwilling to settle down, Betsy pursues adventures for several hundred more pages. She is almost abducted from Westminster by villains, but she is rescued by a viscount; Staple and Trueworth fight for her hand, but Staple eventually concedes. Betsy is attacked by a gallant in a cab on her way home from the theatre; then she is courted by Sir Frederick Fineer, a man of property and class. During this entire time, she has managed to keep Trueworth dangling. She is "indeed a tyrant. . . . She played with her lovers, as she did with her monkey, but expected more obedience from them!—they must look gay or grave, according as she did so . . .; as to the heart, her own being yet untouched, she gave herself but little trouble how that of her lovers stood affected" (2, pp. 228–9). Finally, by the third volume, Trueworth, too, has had enough. Betsy's statement, "whoever thinks to gain me must not be in a hurry" (1, p. 240) has proved to be too true. Not only scandalized by Betsy's friendship with Nancy Forward, the prostitute, but shocked at her receiving gentlemen callers at her lodgings, Trueworth abandons his romantic pursuit and begins instead to court Miss Harriett, Sir Bazil Loveit's daughter. "When he compared the steady temper,—the affability,—the easy, unaffected chearfulness, mixed with a becoming reserve, which that young lady testified in all her words and actions,, with the capricious turns,—the pride, the giddy lightness he had observed in the behavior of Miss Betsy, his admiration of the one was increased by his disapprobation of the other" (3, p. 52). He marries Miss Harriet.

Betsy is undone—momentarily. In a fit of pique, she turns her charms on Fineer until he is exposed by Trueworth as a mere valet. Disguising will not help, and Betsy begins to see her own very real state underneath her thoughtlessness. "When she reflected on the affair of Mr. Trueworth, and the reasons she had given him for speaking and thinking of her in the cool and indifferent manner, she found he now did, she began to be somewhat less tenacious, and acknowledged within herself, that her brother Frank . . . had sufficient cause to blame her conduct. . . . She now saw in their true light all the mistakes she had been guilty of" (3, p. 114).

Foundering, going from one man to another without the balance and proportion of reason, and without Trueworth, Betsy finally agrees to marry Mr. Munden. She is not pleased, however, nor is Mr. Munden happy; quite the contrary: "he was very much disgusted in his mind at her late behaviour;—he found she loved him not and was far from having any violent inclination for her himself" (4, p. 18). Betsy, too, has second thoughts, a premonition of what her future life will be like when she muses, "What can make the generality of Women so fond of marrying?—It looks to me like an infatuation.—Just as if it were not a greater pleasure to be courted, complimented, admired, and addressed by a number, than be confined to one, who from a slave becomes a master, and, perhaps, uses his authority in a manner disagreeable enough" (4, pp. 23–4).

Marry him she does, and so begins the worst period of her trials and character development. Throwing off her flirtatious mein, Betsy quickly adapts herself to her wifely role as advised by Lady Trusty (see 4, pp. 36–8), but she cannot please her husband. "Mr. Munden's notions of marriage had always been extremely unfavourable to the ladies—he considered a wife no more than an upper-servant, bound to study and obey, in all things, the will of him to whom she has given her hand: and how obsequious and submissive soever he appeared when a lover, had fixed his resolution to render himself absolute master when he became a husband" (4, p. 60). He provides her with no pin money, chastizes her expenses for food, and refuses to pay for her servants; marriage has become "an Egyptian Bondage" (4, p. 47). Betsy has no choice but to submit. Cold civility reigns on his part, enforced complaisance on hers. Their married life is not felicitous, but it is bearable until Mr. Munden kills the pet squirrel that Trueworth had given Betsy. "The massacre of so unhurtful a little creature, who never did any thing to provoke its fate, had some thing in it strangely spleenatic and barbarous" (4, p. 63). Munden is revealed in his true colors; no more can a disguise cover his nature. Betsy leaves him, but quickly finds herself in the position of a loose woman in an evil world. She is victimized and exploited even more by the men she meets, and through the arbitration of the Trustys, returns to her husband.

Munden is not content to have just one victim, and when Betsy left, he took a mistress, Mademoiselle de Roquelair. When Betsy learns of her existence, she leaves Munden for good. Her state has

become utterly hopeless, since "a wife who elopes from her husband
forfeits all claim to everything that is his, and can expect nothing
from him till she returns to her obedience" (4, p. 238). But Betsy
will not return; her lawyer tells Mr. Munden that since she is
determined to live apart, "you have no way to preserve her but by
confinement" (4, p. 244). After long consideration, Munden decides
against all the scandal and agrees to a separation, but he will give
her no money.

Betsy has learned quite a lot about the world by this time. When
she hears that Munden is fatally ill, she returns home to nurse him,
as a Christian, not a wife. She is no longer the thoughtless, frivolous
creature of the earlier volumes; she has reached a level of maturity
that allows her to accept her past life and her present duty:

In fine, she now saw herself, and the errors of her past conduct, in their
true light. How strange a creature have I been! . . . how inconsistent
with myself! I knew the character both silly and insignificant; yet did
everything in my power to acquire it:—I aimed to inspire awe and re-
verence in the men; yet, by my imprudence, emboldened them to the
most unbecoming freedoms with me:—I had sense enough to discern real
merit in those who professed themselves my lovers; yet affected to treat
most ill those in whom I found the greatest share of it.—Nature has made
me no fool, yet not one action of my life has given any proof of common
reason.
    Even in the greatest and most serious affair of life—that of marriage
. . . have I not been governed wholly by caprice! I rejected Mr. Trueworth
only because I thought I did not love him enough; yet gave myself to Mr.
Munden, whom I did not love at all; and who has since, alas, taken little
care to cultivate that affection I have laboured to feel for him.
    In summing up this charge against herself, she found that all her faults
and her misfortunes had been owing either to an excess of vanity, a mistaken
pride, or a false delicacy. (4, pp. 159–61)

Meanwhile, Mr. Trueworth has been fortunate enough to perceive
the new, thoroughly reformed Betsy Thoughtless. His own wife
having died, he allows his passion for Betsy to revive, and on the
first anniversary of Munden's death, he arrives in a carriage and six
to claim the widow for his bride.

Unlike predecessors such as Anadea or Placentia, Betsy has learned
about the value of romantic dreams of love; no "shady Grove" and
"purling Stream" for her.[17] Her final acceptance of Trueworth and

his love comes after a long and arduous struggle leading to her understanding the difference between make believe and reality. Betsy and Trueworth must learn that they cannot view the world through romantic spectacles. Betsy is not the flighty, careless, immoral woman who befriends prostitutes, has illegitimate children, and the like. These are some of the stories that are told about her, or that she herself initially subscribes to. Trueworth must learn to see beneath these disguises, just as Betsy must discard the role of heroine and discover the true state of her heart for herself.

Similar to her earlier novels, Haywood uses fiction to reveal the truth. Previously, she exposed the truth only in a hidden fashion. She masked the reality of feminine oppression under the cover of her story; the exterior was racy and inviting, masking the turbulent, rebellious, oppressive interior. In *Betsy Thoughtless,* disguises are employed openly and are put on by the characters as protective devices. The point is still that the mask will be discarded and truth revealed. Masks are stripped from Lady Mellasin, Fineer, Miss Flora, Miss Forward, and Mr. Munden, and their villainous interiors are revealed in much the same fashion as in earlier pieces. Betsy's disguise, however, functions in an opposite fashion; her outward appearance of frivolousness masks the level-headedness that is underneath.

Betsy Thoughtless exemplifies the necessary reconciliation of the contradictory impulses of reason and feeling, reality and appearance that has been a theme in all Haywood's works. As we have seen, it was Betsy's ability to find a balance between these contrasting elements that led to her frequent disasters, and in the end, it was her ability to let reason together with truth triumph that allowed her to succeed.

The History of Jemmy and Jenny Jessamy

The tenets of reason and realism continue to be the basis of Haywood's writing in her next and last novel, *The History of Jemmy and Jenny Jessamy* (1753),[18] which also exhibits Richardson's kitchen morality. It is much more slow-going than its predecessor, *Betsy Thoughtless;* it is also less full of surprises. Both Jenny and Jemmy begin careers of the noblest moral excellence, and it cannot be doubted that their virtue will remain intact and that they will be united at the conclusion.

Jenny, the only daughter and heiress of a wealthy merchant, and Jemmy Jessamy, the only son of a gentleman of good estate, have long been engaged. "It became a kind of second nature in them to love each other, the affection began in infancy, grew up with their years; and if what they felt as they approach'd nearer to maturity did not amount to a passion, it was at least somewhat more than is ordinarily found between a brother and a sister" (1, p. 3). Before their marriage can take place, they are orphaned. Assured of each other's affections, they go to London and using good sense and discretion, enjoy the pleasures of town. They also see so much marital unhappiness and infidelity that they decide to postpone their wedding until, as Jenny says, "we . . . know a little more of the world and of ourselves before we enter into serious matrimony" (1, p. 34). They agree to go their separate ways and observe their friends, and come together to share their perceptions and conclusions. "By this means," Jemmy remarks, "I shall be acquainted with all the humours of your sex, and you no stranger to those of mine; so that neither of us will be at a loss to bear with the foibles which nature or custom may have implanted in the other" (1, p. 42).

The History of Jemmy and Jenny Jessamy is about dispelling illusions. More than any of her other later novels, it is a mature examination of and reflection on all of those beliefs Haywood professed in her earlier novels. It is about the double vision of men and women, and the parallel reality in which women exist. By presenting views through her two protagonists, she underscores this dual perception and the novel recapitulates the fictional technique she used in her earlier works. Her protagonists observe and criticize the illusions that exist in life. What Haywood is at pains to point out is that the examples she uses are proper ones, as they reveal the truth beneath the superficial that Jenny and Jemmy, together with the reader, must discover for themselves.

Their trials begin as Jemmy's false friend, Bellpine, tries to destroy the former's affection for Jenny; he spreads rumors about affairs in which each is said to have been involved. Bellpine himself is an example of this false self that is accepted as the truth. Although he possesses "many accomplishments both natural and acquired . . . [and] knew perfectly how to insinuate himself into the good graces of those he conversed with . . . all his wishes were centered in self-gratification" (1, p. 96), and he makes up stories to suit himself. No matter what evidence she is shown (even a love letter of Jemmy's supposedly written to Miss Chit), Jenny retains her faith in Jemmy's love for her.

Jenny is a rational young woman with a clear view of the kind of relationship she wishes to have with Jemmy: "All I desire is, that when we marry you will either have no amours, or be cautious in concealing them;—and in return, I promise never to examine your conduct, and to send no spies to watch your motions,—to listen to no tales that might be brought me, nor by any methods whatever endeavor to discover more than you would have me" (3, p. 58). After the prescribed number of duels, wounds, tears, and faintings, the lovers are united and live together happily.

But such a summary seems facile and grossly inadequate to convey Haywood's real focus and interest. *The History of Jemmy and Jenny Jessamy* reveals that Haywood no longer sees the great disparity between woman's public and private images that she wrote about in her earlier works. The exploitation and subjugation of females still exists, but the issues appear to have been raised publicly, and Haywood no longer discusses them through subtextual lessons. Jenny is a very open heroine. She finds no need to hide her real meaning in pretense, for her and Jemmy's relationship is based on an almost equal assessment of each other. The realistic evaluation that Haywood undertook in *Betsy Thoughtless* reaches its culmination in the coalescence of fact and fiction, of appearance and reality.

Like fellow novelist, Sarah Fielding, Haywood is concerned with the workings of the mind, especially the female mind. She focuses on the mind's ability to separate out and mix reality and appearance. Bellpine tries to sully Jenny and Jemmy's love for each other by spreading rumors. He tries, in short, to destroy the reality of their love by confusing their minds. Haywood writes, "As it was not in his power to make Jemmy become guilty in fact, his next resource was to make him appear so: to blacken him by any ill report directly to Jenny herself, he knew would be in vain, and treated with contempt by a woman of her penetration; he therefore took a more artful and more sure, tho' slow method of infusing the poison of jealousy and indignation into her soul; he gave it out in whispers, innuendos, and dark hints . . . that Jemmy had an utter aversion to Jenny in his heart" (1, p. 110).

Bellpine's fabrications, rather than uncover, only further mask the truth. Haywood's purpose is to reveal the delusions and false appearance created by untruthful presentations in fiction. Of course,

Bellpine is shown in all his evil and frustrated attempts; and "the good natured reader must certainly be pleased to find, that all the base artifices of Bellpine were so entirely frustrated;—that all his endeavors to dissolve the union between the lovers had only served to cement it more firmly" (2, p. 143). Although virtue is still persecuted, Haywood's note of realism is a strong one on which to end her writing career.

Modern Characters

Haywood's final fictional period includes two short-story collections. The earlier, *Modern Characters* (1753),[19] a work now attributed to Haywood, contains tales advertised as exemplary pieces, good for moral instruction. Rather than stories written in the realistic vein, however, these are tales of sometimes scurrilous passion and intrigue reminiscent of her earlier work. For example, "Lesbia and Sylvius" repeats the seduction of the virtuous Lesbia by Sylvius, who is the "compleat . . . master of dissimulation" (p. 12). Haywood's description of the persecuted innocent is typical and so is Lesbia's downfall. The other "histories" in the collection follow a similar pattern. They show the ugly side of life, including stories of gambling villains ("The Story of Cynthio"), prostitution ("The Story of Marius and Sylvia"), disinterested courtship ("The Story of Mario and Lelia"), the battle of the sexes ("The Story of Lyce and Celsus"), and the results of infidelity ("The Story of Sellius and Meroe"). In the midst of the later, moral, domestic novels, *Modern Characters* is a reversion to Haywood's earlier mode; its stories of romance and passion are similar to those in which she had demonstrated unchallenged mastery, but now there is no attempt to include authorial anger in a covert tale. All the stories of the two volumes of *Modern Characters* are black, depressing vignettes of contemporary people. There is no relief with a good character; all are raped, violated, used.

"The Story of Marius and Sylvia" is a paradigm of this quality. Marius is accused of killing Curtius, and only Sylvia can prove his innocence. She does so, but by lying, she creates an unreal role for herself, and she continues to scheme and to disrupt the world by her untruths. Finally, Sylvia has done so many evil things that she ceases to be a woman at all:

From a sensible and agreeable woman, as she had been in the earlier part of her life, she now was become what she had long affected to be, a creature of a quite different species from the rest of the world; What prostitution had begun, avarice had improved, and resentment had perfected: there only wanted the habit to speak a change of sex in Sylvia. Her face was tann'd with the sun, and purpled with the grape; her voice was become hoarse and rough, fit for the execrations and oaths it was continually pronouncing; and her hands, her stride, her air, all became, not only manly, but like the coarsest of men. (1, pp. 200–01)

Can women only succeed by being transformed into men? Or is Haywood giving us her darkest, grimmest, most desperate virago as an embodiment of her unremitting anger?

Following the popular *Betsy Thoughtless* and *Jemmy and Jenny Jessamy*, *Modern Characters* offers an unmitigated view of destruction and death. Is it possible that Haywood truly saw the world in such a light? Did her numerous novels with their subtle message of rebellion accomplish nothing? Did the fictional world and the real world remain untouched, unchanged? Were women still victimized so openly? Must they still go undercover in order to be saved? A close examination shows that women's position was still one of oppression. Novelists like Haywood in the latter part of the century had to continue to mount their campaign against female suppression and persecution.

The Invisible Spy

The Invisible Spy (1754)[20] by "Exploribus," a pseudonym adopted just this time by Haywood, is another attempt, she writes, "not to ridicule, but reform" (p. 8). The "male" narrator with his cloak of invisibility can "pluck off the mask of hypocrisy from the seeming Saint . . . expose vice and folly in all their various modes and attitudes . . . strip a bad action of all the specious pretences made to conceal or palliate it, and shew it in its native ugliness. At the same time, I have also the means to rescue injured innocence from the cruel attacks begun by envy and scandal, and propagated by prejudice and ill nature. In fine, I am enabled . . . to set both things and persons in their proper colours" (p. 8).

Love continues to be the central theme, but as in the stories from *Modern Characters,* there is a certain negative note about these tales and characters. Rather than disguised anger surfacing in the racy subplots, there is an insidious quality to the work. Her character, Lamia, personifies the tone. She is an elderly lady, supposedly a model of piety and prudence, who becomes a notorious card shark. "She at once degenerated into the very reverse of what she had been, fell into the fashionable follies of the times, at an age when others are beginning to grow weary of them, and commenced a coquette at fifty-five" (1, p. 12). Such a move, counter to nature, is repeated in the cavalcade of stories in *The Invisible Spy;* the tales become attempts to recapture the excitement and expectations of Haywood's earlier romances, and they fail horribly. The bleakness of the work is matched only by *Modern Characters.* In addition, *The Invisible Spy* fails to provide a healthy picture of its own time. Clearly, both are troublesome works, and they leave the reader with an unresolved question concerning Haywood's final assessment of her role as rebel and novelist.

Summary

This period of Haywood's work is characterized by the moral seriousness and sententiousness introduced into fiction by Richardson in 1740. Still adept at giving the public what it wanted, Haywood produced the four-volume novel of moral instruction. With such noteworthy heroines as Betsy and Jenny, she continued to explore the position of women, this time more candidly; her ability to control men and situations is also more evident.

Turning her attention to an examination of her own craft as a writer by analyzing the ubiquitous appearance/reality dichotomy, Haywood has silenced the recurrent termagant that exists in herself, or at least has channeled her aggression into a different mode of expression. In these novels she abandons the double vision, the dual reality that had formed the bulwark of her earlier works. Instead, she tries to combine overt and covert tales in a multidimensional story of women succeeding. With the exception of *Modern Characters* and *The Invisible Spy,* the works of her later period are positive statements about both the condition of women and the state of her art. The novels achieve a tenuous understanding of appearance and reality, of illusion and truth as the reader participates in the moral education of the heroine. Cleomira, Gigantilla, Serinda, and Emanuella have been silenced, and Haywood's final aim is to champion reason and the rational female self.

Chapter Nine

Essays, Periodicals, and Books on Manners

Haywood's fame rests upon her success as a popular novelist. The years from 1719 to 1756 saw her produce over sixty romances, secret histories, and translations of continental romances. During this time, she was also busy writing essays, editing two periodicals, and composing guide books on manners and social behavior. These works, which are fine specimens in their own right, offer further insights into the stylistic and thematic concerns of her earlier and later novels and romances.

Mary Stuart

Haywood's initial attempts to write something other than romances and novels produced two hybrid works, *Mary Stuart* (1725) and *The Tea-Table* (1725). Neither is true fiction, yet neither is free from heavy reliance on fictional techniques.

Mary Stuart, Queen of Scots[1] is offered "not as a Romance, but a True History" (p. iii), and Mary personifies many virtues that Haywood's women readers would do well to emulate; she also illustrates certain evils that should be avoided. Haywood attempts to make Mary's life and deeds into an examplary biography, but she soon loses this moral-guide focus, and the book becomes laced with escapades and elements of romance. Like other Haywood heroines, Queen Mary's experiences include escapes from prison (she is forced to flee from France); exile (she lives in Scotland); an unhappy marriage (Darnley becomes ambitious and scorns her); great love for another man (she falls passionately in love with Bothwell); further imprisonment (she is locked away in Loch Leven Castle); and finally, total deprivation of freedom and life in the Tower of London. The character becomes a romance heroine, and the moral biography but another version of Haywood's endless tale of persecuted innocence.

The Tea-Table

A few months before the publication of *Mary Stuart,* Haywood tried another nonfictional composition, this time in brief essay form; the pieces are Addisonian in style and reflect the sophistication of the city dweller. *The Tea-Table*[2] is also dependent upon fictional props; the contents represent "the Various Foibles, and Affections, which form the Character of an Accomplish'd *Beau,* or a Modern *Fine Lady.* Interspersed with several Entertaining and Instructive Stories." This work resembles *La Belle Assemblée,* part 1, which Haywood had translated the previous year; all of the material in the former could be placed in one of the days found in the latter. The structure of both works is similar: polite conversation, a love-reason debate, a poem, an illustrative story. In other words, it is the usual collection of tales of love and intrigue, and Haywood's initial urbanity is lost amid the passion of stories such as "Beraldus and Celemena; or, the Punishment of Mutability."

Celemena, the illegitimate child of a prince, has an initial aversion to marriage. She goes to live with the Princess of Parma and passes many pleasant hours there "till Love . . . that stealing Poyson of a Woman's Peace, diffus'd itself through all the Veins of the unexperienced Maid" (p. 22); the object of these emotions is Beraldus, "a young Gentleman of but small Fortune" (p. 23). Naive and unsophisticated "she confess'd without Reserve the Tenderness she had for him, indulg'd him in all the Liberties that Modesty wou'd allow; and at last . . . permitted him to transgress those Bounds:— He obtain'd of the believing Maid all she had to give. . . . But this inconstant Rover, the Victory once gain'd, despis'd the too easy Conquest. . . . In *publick* she became the subject of his *Mirth,* and in private of his *Contempt"* (p. 24). Beraldus continues to discredit Celemena while he takes a new mistress, Lamira, whom he marries. Celemena loses rational control and tries to kill Lamira, but fails. Finally, recovering her reason, she begs to be sent to a monastery "where she lingred out a few years of Life in wasting Sorrow" (p. 45). After a few years, Beraldus finds he can tolerate Lamira no longer, and he poisons her and then is put to death himself.

Celemena and her story are presented as a model for moral instruction, the narrator of *The Tea-Table* tells us; she then goes on to assess the story for her readers:

I cannot help saying that I think the Character of *Celemena* faulty.—She yields, in my Opinion, with too much ease, to create that Pity for her Misfortunes, which otherwise they cou'd not fail of exciting.—I wou'd have all Women have a better Excuse for such an Excess of Passion, than merely the agreeable person of a Man. . . . But yet sometimes 'tis necessary . . . to be reminded that there have been Men so base; our Sex is of it self so weak, especially when we suffer what little Share of Reason we have to be debilitated by Passion, that we stand in need of all the Helps we can procure, to defend us from becoming the Victim of our own Softness. (pp. 46–8)

In the second volume of *The Tea-Table,* Haywood abandons the narrative framework and includes a patchwork of verse and prose narratives on the theme of persecuted virtue. Her disregard of formal structure is unfortunate, because the earlier work was beginning to move toward sound characterization. Haywood, however, chose to focus on incident, and the remainder of *The Tea-Table* is a watered-down version of some of her more successful earlier novels.

Haywood herself, however, was convinced that this fictionalized instruction offered by far the best method of inculcating morals. As she says in *The Tea-Table* during a discussion defending novel writing, "we cannot believe that the celebrated Madam D'Anois, Monsieurs Bandell, Scudery, Sergrais . . . Perriers, and many other learned Writers, would have been at the Expence of so much Time and Pains, only for the Pleasure of inventing a Fiction, or relating a Tale.—No, they had other Views.—They had an Eye to the Humours of the Age they liv'd in, and knew that Morals, meerly as Morals, wou'd obtain but slight Regard: to inspire Notions, therefore, which are necessary to reform the Manners, they found it most proper to cloath Instruction with Delight" (p. 49). Thus she too clothes her instruction with delight.

Reflections on Love

Attempting to explore the more philosophical areas of love, Haywood wrote *Reflections on the Various Effects of Love*[3] in 1726. Unlike *The Tea-Table, Reflections* does not try to maintain the illusion of a narrative framework, and each of its tales stands as an independent entity. The stories of Celia and Evandra, for example, represent two aspects of love: revenge and generosity. In another tale, Climene composes model letters to Mirtillo, one telling of his love for her

although he is absent, the other describing his desertion of her and
his consequent lack of love. The stories soon become a more detailed
catalog of love woes similar to those in a scandal novel. Sophiana
has been abandoned by her great love, Aranthus, but she is sought
after by Martius, "a Man of Birth and Fortune and a very great
Courtier" (p. 49). Martius continues to press his suit, and though
Sophiana had made a fool of herself once for love and vows never
to do so again, she quickly is overcome by Martius and his soft
words. When she loses her money and her reputation, however,
Martius abandons her. The narrator concludes, "To have despis'd
Aranthus wou'd have render'd her Praiseworthy, but so suddenly to
become devoted to *Martius* is certainly so great a Proof of Levity as
Nothing can excuse" (p. 54).

All the "reflections" made on the "various effects of love" present
a jaundiced, one-sided view, and the book becomes an indictment
of love's cruelly destructive nature. Haywood remarks, "A Woman,
where she loves, has no Reserve; she profusely gives her All, has no
Regard to any Thing but obliging the Person she affects, and lavishes
her whole Soul" (p. 12). She is utterly consumed by passion and
therefore gives up her reason to love. "But Man, more wisely, keeps
a Part of his for other Views, and he has still an Eye to Interest and
Ambition" (p. 12); man retains a portion of his rational self and
never devotes himself entirely. As she aptly summarizes in *The Tea-
Table,* a double standard concerning men and women and their
relationship to love is clearly marked. For men in love, there is "no
Ruin of Character, no Loss of Fame" (p. 10); woman, on the other
hand, when she "falls a Prey to the rapacious Wishes of her too
dear Undoer, she falls without excuse. Without even Pity for the
Ruin her Inadvertency has brought upon her" (p. 10).

Love-Letters on All Occasions

Both the tender passion—love—and the irrational emotion—
lust—are the focus of Haywood's *Love-Letters on All Occasions Lately
Passed between Persons of Distinction* (1730).[4] It is an amorphous collection of model "occasional" letters written to exemplify the various
situations of lovers that require epistles. Strephon, for example,
writes to Dalinda "on her forbidding him to speak of love" and
"Orontes to Deanira entreating her to give him a meeting." The
letters unfortunately reveal only conventional responses to somewhat

tawdry and mundane situations. They are characterized by excessive use of hyperbole and exaggeration, with nothing to relieve the mawkish sentimentality that arises from the recital of the lovers' woes. There are several series of letters, but by and large, Haywood does not exploit the narrative possibility of this literary form.

One group, letters 13 to 36, is typical of the entire collection. Elismonda has granted Theano the "last Favour" and is now in constant apprehension that Theano will desert her; when he fails to keep an appointment, she is thrown into violent emotional agitation that continues for several letters. Theano is unable to pacify her when he finds that he must leave town in order to settle his estate; Elismonda is again overwhelmed with paroxysms of fear. After more delays and further agonizings, they are united and seem destined to live happily. This series is reminiscent of *Letters from a Lady of Quality to a Chevalier,* but lacks the spontaneity and genuine unconscious revelations found in the earlier work. Elismonda's agitation appears to be conscious artifice, and rather than a serious and mature lover, she remains the coquette. The love she seeks is all exterior, with no deep-rooted, rational foundation.

Haywood will not condone such silly, superficial behavior. In fact, one of the most important things *Love-Letters on All Occasions* does is to define the difference between mere capricious, romantic love and the true, lasting emotion. In letter 1, for example, Darien writes to Climene and tells her how foolish her notion of love is:

But you tell me, that if I lov'd you with that Height of Passion, you would wish to inspire, I should be eternally in Apprehensions of losing you, tremble even at my own Shadow . . . watch your very look, and if I chanc'd but even to imagine you cast one too favourable on any other, show my Resentment to the Man so favour'd, by immediately drawing my Sword; then, fearful of offending you, drop the Point, and, presenting you with the Hilt, beg you on my Knees to plunge it in my Breast, or ease me of the Pain of Doubt!—Why, really, my dear *Climene!* This is a fine sort of Romantic Behaviour; but I can scarce believe the Woman who knows what 'tis to feel a sincere Affection, would wish to find it in the Man she loves.—'Tis a Proof of Vanity and Coquetry to the last Degree. (pp. 2–3)

It is all show, yet, Haywood fears, it is the sort of demonstration most women desire. True love, lasting tenderness and kindness, she has Phyletus write to Delia (letter 2), is "when my working Mind is labouring for your Interest, when, neglecting those Affairs which are immediately my own, all my Thoughts are taken up with yours, when studious for your Happiness alone, I prove it makes the best of mine, and that nothing relating to myself *only* is capable of giving me a Moment's Joy or Grief" (p. 9).

There are a few significant insights concerning the nature of love found in this work, as the majority of the letters cater to the sensational, romantic notions that Climene, Delia, and Elismonda seem set on believing. The letters exhibit more frippery than common sense.

A Present for a Servant Maid

Haywood's *A Present for a Servant Maid; or, the Sure Means of Gaining Love and Esteem* (1743)[5] is in direct contrast to *Love Letters*. It is a sober book written for all future Pamelas. Founded on the idea that "there cannot be a greater Service done to the Commonwealth . . . than to lay down some general Rules for . . . Behavior" (p. 5), it is a compendium of instructions for young ladies in service on "Sloth," "Sluttishness," "Telling Family Affairs," "Directions for Going to Market," "Washing Victuals," "Dressing Meat," "Washing," and "Chastity." Far more than any of Haywood's previous essays, this is an instructive piece.

Although she still counsels that women preserve virtue, Haywood sometimes advises more expedience than maidenly reserve as she tells her readers how to use sexual advances to their own best interest. If the temptation comes from the Master, for example, the girl should reflect on whether or not the Master is married or single, and act accordingly. If he is single,

Let no wanton Smile, or light coquet Air give him room to suspect you are not so much displeased with the Inclination he has for you as you would seem; for if he once imagines you deny but for the sake of Form, it will the more enflame him, and render him more pressing than ever. Let your Answers, therefore, be delivered with the greatest Sedateness; shew that you are truly sorry, and more ashamed than vain, that he finds any thing in you to like. . . . But if you fail in this laudable Ambition, if he persists in his Importunities, and you have Reason to fear he will make Use of other Means than Persuasions to satisfy his brutal Appetite . . . you have nothing to do, but, on the first Symptom that appears of such a Design, to go directly out of his House. (pp. 46–7)

If he is a married man, "you must remonstrate the Wrong he would do his Wife, and how much he demeans both himself and her by making such an Offer to his own Servant" (p. 47). Haywood's final word: "I shall therefore conclude as I began, with exhorting you to make use of the Understanding God has given you, in a serious consideration of the Hints I have thrown together, in order to render you both valuable and happy" (p. 50).

The *Female Spectator*

From April 1744 to May 1746 Haywood anonymously published a monthly journal entitled the *Female Spectator*.[6] It was the first magazine by and for women and, as Whicher notes, was extraordinarily popular.[7] It was actually a collection of essays and is the product of four women:

Mira, a lady descended from a family to which wit seems hereditary, married to a gentleman every way worthy of so excellent a wife, and with whom she lives in . . . perfect harmony. . . . Next . . . a widow of quality, who not having buried her vivacity in the tomb of her lord, continues to make one in all the modish diversions of the times, so far . . . as she finds them consistent with innocence and honour. . . . The third is the daughter of a wealthy merchant, charming as an angel, but endued with so many accomplishments, that to those who know her truly, her beauty is the least distinguished part of her. (1, p. 4)

The fourth is the "Female Spectator" herself.

Like its male predecessor, the *Spectator,* the purpose of Haywood's Addisonian essays and observations was to rectify the manners of the age by castigating its follies. Within the pages of the *Female Spectator,* gambling, lying, jilting, scandal bearing, and the like are discussed as they affect women. Current affairs, wars, and political issues are not "within the province of a Female Spectator:—such as armies marching,—battles fought,—towns destroyed,—rivers crossed, and the like:—I should think it ill became to take up my own readers' time with such accounts as are every day to be found in the public papers" (2, p. 101). Instead, Haywood continues, "To check the enormous growth of luxury, to reform the morals, and improve the manners of an age, by all confessed degenerate and sunk, are the great ends for which these essays were chiefly intended; and the authors flatter themselves that nothing has been advanced, but may contribute in a more or less degree to the accomplishing so glorious a point" (2, pp. 102–3). Topics are introduced frequently by way of a conversation or letter, and the discussion that follows is often illustrated by an anecdote or story. Unlike other essay attempts, the fiction is kept to a minimum, and the *Female Spectator* becomes Haywood's most concentrated attempt to take a serious measure of the morals and mores of her time.

Naturally, the focus is on women and their concerns, principally courtship and marriage. Unlike the revolutionary note sounded in her novels and stories, which urged sweeping changes in the male-dominated situation, here (as in *A Present for a Servant Maid*) Haywood admonishes women to find suitable and acceptable means of survival. For the first time she openly articulates her doctrine of quiet rebellion as she defines woman's role of seeming compliance but actual revolt: "A modest wife should never affect the virago, and for her own sake be wary, even when most provoked, that nothing in her behaviour should bear the least resemblance with such wretches [the prostitutes whom she has just described]. I have in a former *Spectator,* taken notice, that it is not by force our sex can hope to maintain their influence over the men, and I again repeat it as the most infallible maxim, that whenever we would truly conquer, we must seem to yield" (2, p. 179).

Although her focus is on the home (even in the light of her own career, she does not question the validity and rightness of women's place in the home), she strongly argues for women's education, knowledge of the world, and a good marriage coming from the partnership of enlightened participants—a "Sympathy of Humour," which is a product of an educated female and male population.

Haywood's instruction also includes discoveries on the theatre, gaming, gambling, reading, natural philosophy, the use of tea, astronomy, and such qualities as good humor, ingratitude, and taste. The *Female Spectator* thus becomes a compendium of moral instruction, virtuous reading, and practical skills.

The *Parrot*

The response to the *Female Spectator* was so great that Haywood began the *Parrot*[8] on 2 August 1746; it lasted only until 4 October 1746. Designed to be a "Compendium of the times," the *Parrot* consisted of two parts: moralizings on life and manners by a miraculous parrot, and a digest of whatever happenings the author could scrape together. The news of the day was concerned chiefly with the fate of the rebels in the Stuart uprising of 1745 and with rumors of the Pretender's movements.[9] The *Parrot* also found news among the follies of the fair sex and events like the trials of rebels. Reporting the news, however, did not appear to be Haywood's forte, and the *Parrot* quickly degenerated to reporting such pathetic incidents as the death of Jemmy Dawson's sweetheart.[10] Without the moral seriousness and sententiousness of the *Female Spectator,* the work was doomed.

Epistles for the Ladies

Haywood's abortive attempt with the *Parrot* clearly underscored the notion that her own expertise lay not with news reporting, but with a study and recital of the female condition. Thus in 1749 she wrote *Epistles for the Ladies,*[11] a collection of letters markedly different in tone from her earlier efforts, yet returning to her area of proficiency.

Steamy romanticism gives way to praise for woman's long suffering, her endurance of love in the face of a fickle lover, and ultimately, the triumph of her virtue. There is no catering to the public's taste for scandal and passion in *Epistles for the Ladies,* and as Whicher notes, "the balance inclines rather heavily toward sober piety."[12] Similar to Mrs. Rowe's novels, the *Epistles* exudes an air of rationality and respectability. The egregious women of her earlier works are replaced by models of virtuous conduct in an otherwise licentious age. Aminta displays self-possession as she endures the combined treachery of her lover and her most intimate friend; Eusebia discusses the power of divine music with the Bishop; Philenia and Aristander debate the principles of reason and philosophy that govern their existence; and Isabinda composes a song celebrating the happy state of wedlock.

In *Epistles for the Ladies* Haywood does not introduce any new material, and in most instances there is a distinct reworking of old themes: seduction and betrayal, love and hate. But in several of the stories, the women take on a new characteristic: they speak openly and forthrightly, with little need to disguise their sentiments. Palmira writes to Sophronia about her decision to leave her abusing, insulting husband: "I am sometimes fearful . . . that no failures on his part can release me from the obligations I am under of endeavouring to deserve his love, by obeying him in all lawful commands and doing every thing in my power to contribute to his welfare and happiness; but then again I reflect, that the same ordinance which made me a *wife,* was never intended to make me the victim of a *husband*'s unreasonable passions; that *God,* who gave the sovereignty to man, made *woman* a *helpmate,* not a *vassal"* (1, p. 232). Her husband has so violated her with his unprovoked brutality, that Palmira feels justified in leaving him. She is an example of the modern woman and her dilemma: "I am divided within my self . . . which way soever I behave, I can neither satisfy the world nor myself!—Many have thought me too passive, and condemned my want of that proper resentment becoming a woman who knew her conduct to be unblameable; others may, and doubtless so, think I have carried things to too high a pitch" (1, p. 233). Haywood does not agree.

Palmira's problem, and that of many of the women in the *Epistles,* is faulty training. As she had done in the *Female Spectator,* Haywood argues for an improved system of education for women. No matter how careful one's parents are, without an adequately supervised education of the world and its philosophies the young lady will be duped and destroyed by "some gay and self-sufficient coxcomb" (2, p. 200). When addressed in all the splendor of his pretended passion, she will easily fall victim to his rhetoric; she will think herself the goddess he names her and thus assure her fall and destruction. "In a word, too much restraint is as dangerous as too much Liberty.— Let, therefore, the young Corinna see something of the humours of the town" (2, p. 201); her natural good sense coupled with an adequate education will enable her to interpret properly what she sees.

The natural good sense with which she endows Corinna is a hallmark of the majority of women in the *Epistles.* Indeed, the considerable candor in these letters makes it clear that Haywood finds it no longer necessary to hide her real meaning in covert tales; she can address issues openly, and she does so.

The Wife and *The Husband*

Haywood's last known productions, *The Wife,* and *The Husband in Answer to the Wife* (1756),[13] are specifically designed as examples of virtuous behavior for either sex. *The Wife* "contains advice to married women on how to behave toward their husbands in every conceivable situation, beginning with their first few weeks after marriage 'vulgarly call'd the honey-moon,' and ending with 'How a Woman ought to behave when in a state of Separation from her Husband.' "[14] In fact, *The Wife* draws more pictures of the infelicity of marriage than of its bliss. No romance or idyllic scenes interrupt Haywood's steady flow of what she views as reality. Initially assessing the situation, she writes "that one might as well expect to regain lost paradise on this side of the grave as to bring women back to the innocence and simplicity of former times" (p. 4). Their naiveté cannot be recovered, just as that "blissful union of Hearts" (p. 1), marriage, which is the goal and raison d'être of women, cannot be regained when its "love and harmony" have been transformed into cacophonous sounds of "discord and confusion" (p. 2). The prospect looks bleak, but Haywood says that she can offer women guidelines on how to make marriage bearable through the art of disguise. Throughout the piece, she is careful to suggest that the wife must be more than willing to overlook many of her husband's faults and mask her own wishes; only by going more than halfway can she make the relationship successful. Haywood continues, "I would not here be understood, that a women should yield a slavish submission to every unaccountable caprice and whim of the man to whom she is married; or on any force give up her reason and judgment to do him pleasure;—no, that might perhaps be to sin against a more supreme authority than what the law has conferr'd on him;—I would only have her *seem to think* as he does in trifling and insignificant matters, and endeavor to be silent and passive in those of greater importance" (p. 11) (emphasis added).

The passage is important because it stresses the disguise that women must adopt if they are to survive. It must be remembered that it is only a mask; the woman only appears to be passive: "I am far from enjoining, or even approving a passiveness which must render her guilty of wronging her conscience, how misguided soever it may happen to be;—I would only advise her to avoid declaiming against the opinion he maintains; and then I think she may, and ought to vindicate her own, by all the arguments she is able to bring, provided she urges them with meekness and moderation" (p. 16). As in her early tales, the power and force in the relationship still remain with the woman, but she must never demonstrate her control openly. "It therefore behoves every woman, who is desirous of preserving herself in the good graces of her husband, to be very careful how she reports among her friends and acquaintance any ascendancy she has gain'd over him" (p. 105). Secrecy and an ability to keep one's own counsel become the prime qualities in a good wife, for, Haywood stresses, a woman should not deceive herself: in the eighteenth century, it is still a man's world. "The conduct even in the best of husband's, proves that all the fine things they said beforehand were but words of course; the tables, after marriage, are revers'd, the goddess now stripped of all her divinity;—it is no more her province to impose laws, but to receive them;—and happy, very happy may she think herself, whose yoke is soften'd by good nature and indulgence" (p. 203). She continues: "In a word, if she has no reason to believe he likes any other woman so well as herself, and gives her all the marks in his power of a sincere and tender friendship, it is all she ought to expect from him, and that the most beautiful of the sex, after marriage, could ever boast of " (p. 205).

What Haywood gives her readers is a survival kit. *The Wife* is a forthright work. Her basic premise is that man/husband remains the master in the eyes of the world. She teaches women how to live with this world view and turn it to their advantage. Although Haywood would like to believe that "when the two sexes join in the sacred bands of marriage, the woman, from the instant she is made a wife, becomes a co-proprietor with her husband in his fortune" (p. 102), she recognizes the inability of the eighteenth-century to live by such a code. "When a husband perceives his wife begins to interfere in any thing beyond her domestic affairs . . . he presently concludes that she is attempting to infringe on his prerogative" (p. 103), and then he begins to dominate. In an effort to preserve this delicate male ego and retain her own independence, the woman adopts a disguise in order to mask her true feelings. As Haywood concludes, "Secrecy is [such a] very necessary and essential virtue in a married woman, in regard of every thing relating to her husband that she who deviates from it in the least, not only totally destroys her peace of mind, and reputation, but also at the same time loses all the dignity of her own character as a wife" (p. 143).

Similarly in *The Husband* (1756), Haywood carefully and attentively outlines the role and duties a husband must assume in order to attain and maintain a happy marriage:

Methinks a husband would do well, very soon after the object of his wishes loses the name of bride in that of wife, to begin to treat her exactly in the same fashion he resolves to do during his whole life;—the submission and adulations of a lover should be thrown aside, but all the tenderness remain;—he should not, by any word, look, or gesture, give her the least reason either to hope he would be her slave, or to fear he intended to become her master (p. 19).

Haywood continues to admonish the husband and warns him to avoid excessive drinking and womanizing. She instructs him how to behave toward the female servants and finally how to act should his wife prove unfaithful.

But the husband seems unable to learn such basic lessons, and *The Husband,* like *The Wife,* ends with the characters separated and divorced. The majority of chapters in both conduct books focus on the negative aspects of the relationship. Although, as Helene Koon notes, "she continued to turn out novels and essays . . . her work had taken a strongly didactic turn, and morality was less profitable than scandal."[15] Her original, revolutionary notion is not lost. Haywood is still very much concerned in these prose works, especially those of the 1740s and 1750s, to make a realistic assessment of women's position. Her final word, as recorded in *The Wife* and *The Husband,* remains almost as pessimistic as her earlier assessment in *The Perplex'd Dutchess* or *The Mercenary Lover:* woman must still disguise herself as the real source of power.

Chapter Ten
Conclusion

A study of Haywood and her many novels, romances, secret histories, and translations presents a reliable index to the popular fiction of both the early and later years of the eighteenth century. The sheer bulk of her pre-1740 work—sixty-three publications—suggests Haywood's extraordinary popularity. More important still, her work reflects the social, economic, moral, and political ethos that formed the background of what we now recognize as the eighteenth-century novel. The sheer abundance of her works and their popular appeal require that we regard them as significant in the early development of English fiction, while their relationship to really important novels of the period makes them of more than just passing interest. Indeed, Eliza Haywood was surely not just another person churning out romances, as has always been thought. She was an aggressive writer, making important comments upon the position and role of women and their source of power, and an able story-teller whose tales of passion and strife quite understandably caught the fancy of the new novel-reading public.

Haywood's romances that concentrated on the heroine's dilemmas and problems of self-division are a paradigm of female behavior during this time. We cannot say that she very often achieves genuine psychological penetration, but her stories are usually told with considerable narrative energy, detailing the plight of a woman beset or at least perplexed by a world indifferent if not hostile to her as a person. The pattern of conflict varies from tale to tale, but the sheer repetition of the theme in the works of Haywood and Fielding, Inchbald, Smith, and others may have given it validity for women readers conscious of similar tensions in real life. Haywood surely enriches our understanding of those great novels of her period—Richardson's *Pamela* and *Clarissa* especially—that undertake to study some of the same issues, especially the notion of female power, that engaged her attention for so many years. Richardson's story of Pamela Andrews provides a model of proper behavior for a young girl, while Clarissa is the first truly tragic heroine. Both characters become examples of the new breed of women who are independent seekers after personal freedom and identity. On a more mythic scale, they embody the same quest for female identity and striving for personal control that Haywood's heroines represent on a less formal, more popular level.

Haywood's popular novels are important documents not only of women's history, but of literary, social, and moral tensions of their age, tensions generated by the collision of aristocratic tradition with self-righteous middle-class aspiration, of reason with feeling, of male supremacy with a barely emerging but significant sense of womanhood.

Notes and References

Chapter One

1. James Sterling, "To Mrs. Eliza Haywood, On her Writings," in *The Force of Nature; or, The Lucky Disappointment* (London, 1725).

2. David Erskine Baker, Haywood's first biographer, in his *Companion to the Play House* (1764), hints that Haywood herself suppressed the facts of her life "from a supposition of some improper liberties being taken with her character after death by the intermixture of truth and falsehood with her history."

3. George Frisbie Whicher, *The Life and Romance of Mrs. Eliza Haywood* (New York: Columbia University Press, 1915), p. 2, note 3. London Parish Registers contain no information about the birth of one Eliza Fowler in 1693; however, there is a record that "Elizabeth dau. of Robert Fowler and Elizabeth his wife" was christened on 21 January 1689; hence, one's hesitancy to assign 1693 as her certain birthdate.

4. Whicher, *Life,* p. 2, note 4.

The [Rev. Mr. Haywood] was the author of *An Examination of Dr. Clarke's Scripture-Doctrine of the Trinity, with a Confutation of it* (1719). The work is a paragraph-by-paragraph refutation of the *Scripture Doctrine of the Trinity* (1712) by the metaphysical Dr. Samuel Clarke, whose unorthodox views prevented Queen Caroline from making him Archbishop of Canterbury. Haywood was upon safe ground in attacking a book already condemned in Convocation.

5. Ibid., p. 2.

6. Ibid., p. 3, note 5.

7. Ibid., pp. 10–11.

8. Edmund Gosse, *Gossip in a Library* (London: William Heinemann, 1891), pp. 62–63.

9. Ian Watt, *The Rise of the Novel. Studies in Defoe, Richardson, and Fielding* (Berkeley: University of California Press, 1957), p. 44.

10. Jerry C. Beasley, "English Fiction in the 1740s: Some Glances at the Major and Minor Novels," *Studies in the Novel,* 5 (Summer 1973): 161. See also Ruth Perry, *Women, Letters and the Novel* (New York: AMS Press, 1980).

11. Barbara Bellow Watson, "On Power and the Literary Text," *Signs,* 1 (1975–76): 113.

120   ELIZA HAYWOOD

12. Nancy K. Miller, "Emphasis Added: Plots and Plausibilities in Women's Fiction," *PMLA*, 96 (January 1981):46.
13. See Elaine Showalter, *A Literature of their Own. British Women Novelists From Brontë to Lessing* (Princeton: Princeton University Press, 1977), esp. pp. 3–37.
14. Virginia Woolf, "Jane Austen," in *The Common Reader* (New York: Harcourt Brace Jovanovich, 1925), p. 142.
15. Whicher, *Life*, pp. 24–25.

Chapter Two

1. *The Fair Captive: A Tragedy* (London: Printed for T. Jauney and H. Cole, 1721).
2. *A Wife To be Lett: A Comedy*, 2nd ed. (London: Printed for D. Browne, Jr. and sold by J. Osborn, 1729).
3. *Frederick, Duke of Brunswick-Lunenburgh. A Tragedy* (London: Printed for W. Mears and J. Brindley, 1729).
4. *The Opera of Operas; or, Tom Thumb the Great* (London: Printed for William Rayner, 1733).

Chapter Three

1. According to William H. McBurney, *Love in Excess* shares with Swift's *Gulliver's Travels* and Defoe's *Robinson Crusoe* "the distinction of being the most popular English fiction of the eighteenth century before *Pamela.*" "Mrs. Penelope Aubin and the Early Eighteenth-century English Novel," *Huntington Library Quarterly*, 20 (May 1957):250.
2. Sterling, "To Mrs. Eliza Haywood."
3. Bridget G. MacCarthy, *Women Writers. Their Contributions to the English Novel, 1621–1744* (New York: William Salloch, 1948), pp. 140–41.
4. Ibid., p. 141.
5. Ibid., pp. 145–46.
6. *Love in Excess; or, The Fatal Enquiry*, in *The Works of Mrs. Eliza Haywood; Consisting of Novels, Letters, Poems, and Plays*, 4 vols. (London: Printed for Dan. Brown, Jr. and Sam. Chapman, 1724).
7. Whicher, *Life*, p. 36.
8. Ibid., p. 35.
9. R. F. Brissenden, *Virtue in Distress, Studies in the Novel of Sentiment from Richardson to Sade* (New York: Barnes & Noble, 1974), p. 77.
10. Patricia Meyer Spacks, *Imagining a Self. Autobiography and Novel in Eighteenth-century England* (Cambridge: Harvard University Press, 1976), p. 63.
11. Ibid., p. 65.
12. *The British Recluse; or, The Secret History of Cleomira, Suppos'd dead*, in *Secret Histories, Novels, and Poems*, 3d ed. (London: Printed for A. Bet-

tesworth, C. Hitch, D. Browne, T. Astley, and T. Green, 1732), vol. 2.

13. *The Injur'd Husband; or, The Mistaken Resentment. A Novel*, in *Secret Histories, Novels, and Poems*, 3d ed., vol. 2.

14. *Idalia; or, The Unfortunate Mistress*, in *Secret Histories, Novels, and Poems, Written by Mrs. Haywood*, 2d ed. (London: Printed for Dan Browne, Jr. and Sam. Chapman, 1725), vol. 3.

15. One should note that the majority of Haywood's heroines are very active; their adventures and exploits carry them to many foreign countries. These journeys indicate the extensiveness of the evil and persecution with which they must battle. See John J. Richetti, *Popular Fiction Before Richardson. Narrative Patterns 1700–1739* (Oxford: Clarendon Press, 1969), chapter 1.

16. *Lasselia; or, The Self-Abandon'd*, in *Secret Histories, Novels, and Poems*, 3d ed., vol. 4.

17. *The Rash Resolve; or, the Untimely Discovery* (1723; reprint, New York: Garland Publishing, 1973).

Chapter Four

1. Daniel Defoe, *The History of the Life and Adventures of Mr. Duncan Campbell*, 2d ed. (London: Printed for E. Curll, 1720).

2. Mrs. Haywood's association with Aaron Hill and his circle probably led to her introduction to William Bond; Bond was playing the part of Steele to Hill's Addison in *The Plain Dealer*. See Whicher, *Life*, p. 80.

3. *A Spy upon the Conjuror; or, A Collection of Surprising Stories* (London: Printed for Campbell & Burton, 1724).

4. Whicher attributes *A Spy* to Haywood because the passages about love "are in substance and style after Eliza Haywood's manner, while the experiences therein hinted at do not differ essentially from the circumstances of her own life" (p. 83).

5. *The Dumb Projector: Being a Surprizing Account of a Trip to Holland made by Mr. Duncan Campbell* (London: Printed for W. Ellis, J. Roberts, Mrs. Billingsley, A. Dodd, and J. Fox, 1725).

6. Defoe, *Secret Memoirs of the late Mr. Duncan Campbell* (London: 1732).

7. Whicher, *Life*, p. 89.

8. James Sterling, "To Mrs. Eliza Haywood."

Chapter Five

1. *Letters from a Lady of Quality to a Chevalier*, in *The Works of Mrs. Eliza Haywood*, 2d ed. (London: Printed for Dan. Browne, Jr. and Sam. Chapman, 1724), vol. 3.

2. In a "Discourse Concerning Writings of this Nature," an essay appended to the *Letters*, Haywood attempts to assess the struggle undergone by every woman in love:

> In this pleasing, but destructive Amusement, we lose our selves so long, that the return of Reason is too weak to drive it from our Minds; we *wake* indeed from the deluding Dream, but the re- membrance of it lasts; and *Doubts* and *Terrors*, mingling with *Hopes* and *Wishes*, make an eternal War within our bosoms. . . . So this unfortunate Lady, divided between Excess of Love, and Nicety of Honour, could neither resolve to give a loose to the one, nor entirely obey the Precepts of the other, but suffered herself to be tossed alternately by both. And tho' the Person she loved was most certainly . . . deserving all the Condescensions a Woman could make, by his Assiduity, Constancy, and Gratitude, yet it must be a good while before she could receive those Proofs; and the Disquiets she suffered in that time of Probation, were, I think, if no worse ensued, too clear a Price for the Pleasure of being beloved by the most engaging and most charming of his Sex. (p. 7)

3. *La Belle Assemblée; or, The Adventures of Six Days*, 2d ed. (London: Printed for D. Browne, Jr. and S. Chapman, 1725).

4. *L'Entretien des Beaux Esprits* (London: Printed for F. Cogan and J. Nourse, 1734).

5. *The Lady's Philosopher's Stone; or, The Caprices of Love and Destiny* (London: Printed for D. Browne, Jr. and S. Chapman, 1725).

6. *Love in its Variety* (London: Printed for W. Feales and J. Jackson, 1727).

7. *The Disguis'd Prince; or, The Beautiful Parisian* (London: Printed for T. Corbett, 1728).

8. *The Busy-Body; or, Successful Spy*, 2 vols. (London, 1752).

9. *The Virtuous Villager; or, Virgin's Victory*, 2 vols. (London: Printed for Francis Cogan, 1742).

10. Whicher, *Life*, p. 152.

11. See Robert B. Pierce, "Moral Education in the Novel of the 1750s," *Philological Quarterly*, 44 (1965):73–87.

Chapter Six

1. May 1725: *The Tea-Table*, Part 1; *The Dumb Projector; Fatal Fondness*. September 1726: *The Court of Carimania; Letters from the Palace of Fame*. August 1728: *The Disguis'd Prince; Persecuted Virtue*. January 1729: The Agreeable Caledonian; The Fair Hebrew.

2. *The Masqueraders; or, Fatal Curiosity*, in *Secret Histories, Novels, and Poems*, 3d ed., vol. 4.

3. *The Fatal Secret; or, Constancy in Distress,* in *Secret Histories, Novels, and Poems,* 2d ed., vol. 3.

4. *The Surprise; or, Constancy Rewarded,* in *Secret Histories, Novels, and Poems,* 2d ed., vol. 2.

5. *The Arragonian Queen: A Secret History,* 2d ed. (London: Printed for J. Roberts, 1724).

6. *Fantomina; or, Love in a Maze,* in *Secret Histories, Novels, and Poems,* 2d ed., vol. 3.

7. *The City Jilt; or, The Alderman Turn'd Beau: A Secret History* (London: Printed for J. Roberts, 1726).

8. *The Force of Nature; or, The Lucky Disappointment,* in *Secret Histories, Novels, and Poems,* 3d ed., vol. 4.

9. *The Unequal Conflict; or, Nature Triumphant* (London: Printed for J. Walthoe and J. Crokatt, 1725).

10. *Fatal Fondness; or, Love its own Opposer* (London: Printed for J. Walthoe and J. Crokatt, 1725).

11. *The Distressed Orphan; or, Love in a Mad House* (London: Printed for Sabine and Son, 1726). The novel exhibits indebtedness to the theater, specifically the madhouse scenes from Middleton's *The Changling.*

12. *The Mercenary Lover; or, the Unfortunate Heiresses* (1726; reprint New York: Garland Publishing, 1973).

13. *The Double Marriage; or, The Fatal Release,* 3d ed. (London: Printed for J. Roberts, 1726).

14. *Memoirs of a Certain Island Adjacent to the Kingdom of Utopia,* 2d ed. (London: Printed for the Booksellers of London and Westminster, 1726), 2 vols.

15. *Bath Intrigues: in Four Letters to a Friend,* 2d ed. (London: Printed for J. Roberts, 1725).

16. *Memoirs of the Baron de Brosse* (London: Printed for D. Browne, and S. Chapman, 1724). The novel tells the tragic story of the Baron's unsuccessful love attempts to capture the hard-hearted beauty, Larissa, who is not interested in the Baron because she is intriguing with de Monbray. She finally marries yet another count, and de Brosse is plunged into despair; he can barely muster enough strength to defend himself from a false accusation made by de Monbray. He wins his point, however, and the story ends.

17. *The Secret History of the Present Intrigues of the Court of Carimania* (1726: reprint New York: Garland Publishing, 1972).

18. *Letters from the Palace of Fame* (London: Printed for J. Roberts, 1727). Seduction, rapes, and betrayals form the basis of this example of the roman à clef. Its tenuous story soon evaporates into scandal and gossip. Without a key, it is impossible to identify the characters, and the lack of

depth with which they are portrayed makes this the weakest of Haywood's works.

Chapter Seven

　　1. *Cleomelia; or, The Generous Mistress,* 2d ed. (London: Printed for J. Millan and J. Roberts, 1727).
　　2. Haywood's thinking is akin to Clara Reeve's notions of the romance and the novel. As she writes in *The Progress of Romance* (1785):

> The Romance is an heroic fable, which treats of fabulous persons and things.—The novel is a picture of real life and manners, and of the times in which it is written. The Romance in lofty and elevated language describes what never happened nor is likely to happen.— The Novel gives a familiar relation of such things, as pass every day before our eyes, such as may happen to our friend, or to ourselves; and the perfection of it, is to represent every scene, in so easy and natural a manner, and to make them appear so probable, as to deceive us into a persuasion (at least while we are reading) that all is real, until we are affected by the joys or distresses, of the persons in the story, as if they were our own.

Both Reeve and Haywood are concerned with the reality, the true picture of "life as it is lived" that is the province of the novel. Haywood takes this theory one step further as she simultaneously explores the image created by the dominant male and the life lived by the subordinate female.
　　3. *The Fruitless Enquiry,* in *A Collection of Novels,* ed. Mrs. Griffith (London: Printed for G. Kearsley, 1777), vol. 2.
　　4. As Miramillia searches for one happy woman, she hears only tales of unhappiness and disquiet from the women she encounters. For example, Anziana is married against her will and continually mourns her lost lover; Montrana suffers shipwreck, imprisonment, and starvation before being united with his beloved wife, Iseria, who had suffered even more because of his absence; Stenoclea, after much delay, is allowed to marry her lover only to learn that he murdered her brother; Maria wins the affections of the Marquis de Salvilado and discovers that he is an impostor and therefore not worthy of her love; Violathia endures the cruelties of a jealous husband; and Fellisinda must watch a bastard son usurp the place and inheritance of her rightful son. No woman, Miramillia learns, is happy. Discontent, abuse, and disrespect appear to be woman's lot, and Miramillia cries out: "Heavens! . . . are all our Sex devoted to disquiet? Is there a fate upon us to be wretched? Must we labour under woes for our own formation, when Fortune contributes all she can to make us happy?" (p. 255).
　　5. *The Life of Madam de Villesache* (London: Printed for W. Feales and J. Roberts, 1727).

6. *Philidore and Placentia; or, L'Amour trop Delicat,* in *Four Before Richardson. Selected English Novels, 1720–1727,* ed. William H. McBurney (Lincoln: University of Nebraska press, 1963).

7. *The Perplex'd Dutchess; or, Treachery Rewarded,* 2d ed. (London: Printed for J. Roberts, 1728).

8. *The Padlock; or, No Guard without Virtue,* in *The Mercenary Lover; or, The Unfortunate Heiresses,* 3d ed. (London: Printed for N. Dobbs, 1728).

9. *Irish Artifice; or, The History of Clarina,* in *The Female Dunciad,* ed. Edmund Curll (London: Printed for T. Read, 1728).

10. *Persecuted Virtue; or, The Cruel Lover* (London: Printed for J. Brindley and Mr. Whitridge, 1728).

11. *The Agreeable Caledonian; or, Memoirs of Signiora di Morella* (1728; reprint New York: Garland Publishing, 1973).

12. *The Fair Hebrew; or, a True, but Secret History of Two Jewish Ladies,* 2d ed. (London: Printed for J. Brindley, W. Meadows, J. Walthoe, et al., 1729).

13. *The Adventure of Eovaai, Princes of Ijaveo* (1736; reprint New York: Garland Publishing, 1972).

14. *The Adventures of Eovaai* is also a political satire. The character of Ochihatou is a thinly disguised portrait of the hated prime minister, Sir Robert Walpole.

Chapter Eight

1. The annotations of *The Dunciad,* Variorum edition, note that in Pope's attack on Haywood "is exposed, in the most contemptuous manner, the profligate licentiousness of those shameless scribblers (for the most part of that sex, which ought least to be capable of such malice or impudence) who in libellous Memoirs and Novels, reveal the faults and misfortunes of both sexes, to the ruin of public fame or disturbance or private happiness." Elwin and Courthope, *Pope* (London: Printed for the Booksellers, 1729), vol. 4, p. 141.

2. The following passage from *Memoirs of the Court of Lilliput,* p. 16, is a debate between the Lilliputian ladies who were seen by Gulliver in a rather awkward state of undress. They are concerned lest their reputations be compromised.

And besides, the inequality of our Stature rightly consider'd, ought to be for us as full a Security from Slander, as that between Mr. Pope, and those *great* ladies who do nothing without him; admit him to their Closets, their bed-sides, consult him in the choice of their Servants, their Garments, and make no scruple of putting them on or off before him: Every body knows they are Women of strict Virtue, and he a harmless Creature, who has neither the Will, nor

Power of doing any farther Mischief than with his Pen, and that he seldom draws, but in defense of their Beauty; or to second their Revenge against some presuming Prude, who boasts a Superiority of Charms: or in privately transcribing and passing for his own, the elaborate Studies of some more learned Genius.

3. Whicher, *Life,* pp. 125–26.
4. Whicher, *Life,* p. 128, notes, "Of her forty publications before 1728 only fifteen, of which five from their libelous nature could not be acknowledged, failed to sail openly under her colors."
5. *Anti-Pamela; or, Feign'd Innocence detected in a Series of Syrena's Adventures,* 2d ed. (London: Printed for F. Cogan, 1742).
6. An example of Syrena's machinations is found in the following scene:

The young Deceiver . . . had no sooner left the Chamber, than she tore her Hair and Cloaths, pinch'd her Arms and Hands till they became black; pluck'd down one of the Curtains from the Bed, and throw'd it on the Floor, and put her self and every thing in such Disorder, that the Room seem'd a Scene of Distraction—Then having watch'd at the Window Mr. L——'s going out, she rung the Bell with all her Strength, and the Maids below came running up, surpriz'd what could be the meaning, but were more so, when they saw *Syrena* in the most pity-moving Posture imaginable—She was lying cross the Bed, her Eyes rolling as just recover'd from a Fit—She wrung her Hands—She cry'd to Heaven for Justice—She rav'd, as if the Anguish of her Mind had deprived her of Reason.—The Girls were strangely alarm'd at so unexpected a Sight—and ask'd her the Occasion—but instead of giving any direct Answer, she only cry'd, let me go—O let me get out of this accursed, this fatal House. . . . she started up, and snatching a Penknife that lay upon the Table, cry'd she would run it into her Heart, if they offer'd to detain her . . . and in spite of all they could do, broke from them and ran down Stairs and so into the Street . . . where she soon got a Coach, and was carry'd to her Mother's; who highly applauded her Management of this Affair. (pp. 95–96)

7. *The Fortunate Foundlings* (Dublin: Printed for A. Bradley, 1744).
8. Whicher, *Life,* p. 152.
9. *Life's Progress through the Passions; or, The Adventures of Natura* (London: Printed for T. Gardner, 1748).
10. *Dalinda; or, The Double Marriage* (London: Printed for C. Corbett and G. Woodfall, 1749).
11. Whicher, *Life,* p. 94.

12. *A Letter from H——— G———g, Esq., One of the Gentlemen of the Bedchamber of the young Chevalier* (London: Printed at Royal Exchange, Temple-Bar, Charing Cross, 1750).

13. *The History of Cornelia* (London: A. Millar, 1750).

14. Whicher, *Life,* p, 158.

15. *The History of Miss Betsy Thoughtless* (1751; reprint New York: Garland Publishing, 1979), 4 vols.

16. Whicher, *Life,* p. 158.

17. See dedication to *The Fatal Secret.*

18. *The History of Jemmy and Jenny Jessamy* (London: J. Gardner, 1753).

19. *Modern Characters* (London: Printed for T. Gardner, 1753), 2 vols.

20. *The Invisible Spy. By Exploribus* (London: Harrison and Co., 1755), 2 vols.

Chapter Nine

1. *Mary Stuart, Queen of Scots,* 2d ed. (London: Printed for D. Browne, Jr. and S. Chapman, J. Woodman, D. Lyon, 1726).

2. *The Tea-Table; or, A Conversation between some Polite Persons of both Sexes, at a Lady's Visiting Day* (London: Printed for J. Roberts, 1725).

3. *Reflections on the Various Effects of Love,* 2d ed. (London: Printed for N. Dobb, 1726).

4. *Love-Letters on All Occasions Lately passed between Persons of Distinction* (London: Printed for J. Brindley, R. Willock, J. Jackson, J. Penn, and F. Cogan, 1730).

5. *A Present for a Servant Maid; or, the Sure Means of gaining Love and Esteem* (Dublin: George Faulkner, 1743).

6. Mary Priestley, ed., *The Female Spectator, Being Selections from Mrs. Eliza Haywood's Periodical (1744–1746)* (London: Bodley Head, 1929).

7. Whicher, *Life,* p. 141: "Twenty-four numbers—two months were omitted—were bound in four volumes upon completion of the series and sold with such vigor that an edition labeled the third was issued at Dublin in 1747."

8. *Parrot. With a Compendium of the Times* (London: Printed for T. Gardner, 1746).

9. Whicher, *Life,* p. 145.

10. Whicher, *Life,* p. 145.

11. *Epistles for the Ladies,* 3d ed. (London: Printed for H. Gardner, 1776).

12. Whicher, *Life,* p. 138.

13. *The Wife* (London: Printed for T. Gardner, 1756). *The Husband. In Answer to the Wife* (London: Printed for T. Gardner, 1756).

14. Whicher, *Life,* pp. 147–48.

15. Helene Koon, "Eliza Haywood and *The Female Spectator,"* *Huntington Library Quarterly,* 42 (1978):44.

Selected Bibliography

PRIMARY SOURCES

Adventures of Eovaai, Princes of Ijaveo. Printed for S. Baker, 1736.

The Agreeable Caledonian; or, Memoirs of Signiora di Morella, a Roman Lady. Printed for R. King and sold by W. Meadows, T. Green, J. Stone, J. Jackson, and J. Watson, 1728, 1729.

The Arragonian Queen: A Secret History. Printed for J. Roberts, 1724.

Bath Intrigues: in four Letters to a Friend in London. Printed for J. Roberts, 1725.

La Belle Assemblée; or, the Adventures of Six Days. Being a Curious Collection of Remarkable Incidents which happen'd to some of the First Quality in France (trans.). Printed for D. Browne, Jr., and S. Chapman, 1724.

The British Recluse; or, the Secret History of Cleomira, Suppos'd Dead. Printed for D. Browne, Jr., W. Chetwood and J. Woodman; and S. Chapman, 1722.

The City Jilt; or, the Alderman Turn'd Beau. A Secret History. Printed for J. Roberts, 1726.

Cleomelia; or, the Generous Mistress. Printed for J. Millan and sold by J. Roberts, T. Astley, W. Meadows, J. Mackeuen, H. Northcock, 1727.

Dalinda; or, the Double Marriage. Printed for C. Corbett and G. Woodfall, 1749.

The Disguis'd Prince; or, the Beautiful Parisian (trans.). Printed for T. Corbett and sold by J. Roberts, 1728, 1729.

The Distress'd Orphan; or, Love in a Mad-house. Printed for J. Roberts, 1726.

The Double Marriage; or, the Fatal Release. Printed for J. Roberts, 1726.

The Dumb Projector: Being a Surprizing Account of a Trip to Holland made by Mr. Duncan Campbell. Printed for W. Ellis, J. Roberts, Mrs. Billingsly, A. Dodd, and J. Fox, 1725.

L'Entretien des Beaux Esprits. Being the Sequel to La Belle Assemblée (trans.). Printed for F. Cogan and J. Nourse, 1734.

Epistles for the Ladies. Printed for T. Gardner, 1749, 1750.

The Fair Captive: A Tragedy. Printed for T. Jauncy and H. Cole, 1721.

The Fair Hebrew; or, a True, but Secret History of Two Jewish Ladies. Printed for J. Brindley, W. Meadows and J. Walthoe, A. Bettesworth, T. Astley, T. Worral, J. Lewis, J. Penn, and R. Walker, 1729.

Fantomina; or, Love in a Maze. Printed for D. Browne, Jr., and S. Chapman, 1725.

Fatal Fondness; or, Love its own Opposer. Printed for J. Walthoe and J. Crokatt, 1725.

The Fatal Secret; or, Constancy in Distress. Printed for J. Roberts, 1724.

The Female Spectator. Printed for T. Gardner, 1745.

The Force of Nature; or, the Lucky Disappointment: A Novel. Included in editions of *Secret Histories,* etc.

The Fortunate Foundlings. Printed for T. Gardner, 1744.

Frederick, Duke of Brunswick-Lunenburgh. A Tragedy. Printed for W. Mears and J. Brindley, 1729.

The Fruitless Enquiry. Being a Collection of Several Entertaining Histories and Occurrences, Which Fell under the Observation of a Lady in her Search after Happiness. Printed for J. Stephens, 1727.

The History of Cornelia. Printed for A. Millar, 1750.

The History of Jemmy and Jenny Jessamy. Printed for T. Gardner, 1753.

The History of Miss Betsy Thoughtless. Printed for T. Gardner, 1751.

The Husband. In Answer to The Wife. Printed for T. Gardner, 1756.

Idalia; or, the Unfortunate Mistress. Printed for D. Browne, Jr., W. Chetwood, and S. Chapman, 1723.

The Injur'd Husband; or, the Mistaken Resentment. A Novel. Printed for D. Browne, Jr., W. Chetwood and J. Woodman, and S. Chapman, 1723.

The Invisible Spy. By Exploribus. Printed for T. Gardner, 1755.

Irish Artifice; or, The History of Clarina, in *The Female Dunciad.* Printed for T. Read, 1728.

The Lady's Philosopher's Stone; or, The Caprices of Love and Destiny: an Historical Novel (trans.). Printed for D. Browne, Jr., and S. Chapman, 1725.

Lasselia; or, the Self-Abandon'd. Printed for D. Browne, Jr., and S. Chapman, 1723.

A Letter from H—— G——, Esq. One of the Gentlemen of the Bedchamber to the Young Chevalier. Printed and sold at the Royal-Exchange, Temple-Bar, Charing Cross, and all the Pamphlet Shops of London and Westminster, 1750.

Letters from a Lady of Quality to a Chevalier (trans.). Printed for W. Chetwood, 1721.

Letters from the Palace of Fame. Printed for J. Roberts, 1727.

The Life of Madam de Villesache. Printed for W. Feales and sold by J. Roberts, 1727.

Life's Progress through the Passions; or, the Adventures of Natura. Printed for T. Gardner, 1748.

Love in Excess; or, the Fatal Enquiry. Printed for W. Chetwood and J. Roberts, 1719.

Love in its Variety: Being a Collection of Select Novels (trans.). Printed for W. Feales and J. Jackson, 1727.

Love-Letters on All Occasions Lately Passed between Persons of Distinction. Printed for J. Brindley, R. Willock, J. Jackson, J. Penn and F. Cogan, 1730.

Mary Stuart, Queen of Scots (trans.). Printed for D. Browne, Jr., S. Chapman, J. Woodman, and D. Lyon, 1725.

The Masqueraders; or, Fatal Curiosity: being the Secret History of a Late Amour. Printed for J. Roberts, 1724.

Memoirs of a Certain Island Adjacent to the Kingdom of Utopia. Printed for the Booksellers of London and Westminster, 1725, 1726.

Memoirs of the Baron de Brosse. Printed for D. Browne, Jr., and S. Chapman, 1725, 1726.

The Mercenary Lover; or, the Unfortunate Heiresses. Printed for N. Dobb, 1726.

Modern Characters. Printed for T. Gardner, 1753. 2 vols.

The Opera of Operas; or, Tom Thumb the Great. Printed for W. Rayner, 1733.

The Padlock; or, No Guard Without Virtue. In *The Mercenary Lover,* 3d ed. Printed for N. Dobb, 1728.

The Parrot. With a Compendium of the Times. Printed for T. Gardner, 1746.

The Perplex'd Dutchess; or, Treachery Rewarded. Printed for J. Roberts, 1728.

Persecuted Virtue; or, The Cruel Lover. Printed for J. Brindley and sold by W. Meadows and H. Whitridge, T. Worral, R. Francklin, and J. Watson, 1728.

Philidore and Placentia; or, L'Amour trop Delicat. Printed for T. Green and sold by J. Roberts, 1727.

Poems on Several Occasions. Included with no separate title page in Haywood's *Works,* 1724.

A Present for a Servant-Maid; or, the Sure Means of Gaining Love and Esteem. Printed for T. Gardner, 1743.

The Rash Resolve; or, the Untimely Discovery. Printed for D. Browne, Jr., and S. Chapman, 1724.

Reflections on the Various Effects of Love, According to the contrary Dispositions of the Persons on whom it operates. Printed for N. Dobb, 1726.

Secret Histories, Novels, and Poems. Printed for D. Browne, Jr., and S. Chapman, 1725, 1732, 1742.

The Secret History of the Present Intrigues of the Court of Carimania. Printed for the Booksellers of London and Westminster, 1727.

Secret Memoirs of the late Mr. Duncan Campbell, the Famous Deaf and Dumb Gentlemen. Printed for J. Millan and J. Chrichley, 1732.

A Spy upon the Conjuror; or, A Collection of Surprising Stories. Printed for T. Corbet, 1724.

The Surprise; or, Constancy Rewarded. Printed for J. Roberts, 1724.

The Tea-Table; or, A Conversation between some Polite Persons of both Sexes, at a Lady's Visiting Day. Printed for J. Roberts, 1725.

The Unequal Conflict; or, Nature Triumphant. Printed for J. Walthoe and J. Crokatt, 1725.

The Virtuous Villager; or, Virgin's Victory (trans.). Printed for F. Cogan, 1742.

The Wife. Printed for T. Gardner, 1756.

A Wife To be Lett: A Comedy. Printed for D. Browne, Jr., and S. Chapman, 1724.

The Works of Mrs. Eliza Haywood; Consisting of Novels, Letters, Poems, and Plays. Printed for D. Browne, Jr., and S. Chapman, 1724.

WORKS PUBLISHED BY HAYWOOD

The Busy-Body; or, Successful Spy, 1742.

Anti-Pamela; or, Feign'd Innocence detected, in a Series of Syrena's Adventures, 1741.

SECONDARY SOURCES

Beasley, Jerry C. "English Fiction in the 1740s: Some Glances at the Major and Minor Novels." *Studies in the Novel,* 5 (Summer 1973):155–76. Beasley argues that the fiction of the 1740s presents a new moral focus; heroism is translated into contemporary terms and there is an increasing importance put on the individual man or woman.

————. "Romance and the 'New' Novels of Richardson, Fielding and Smollett." *Studies in English Literature,* 16 (1976):437–50. The major novels of the 1740s are essentially circumstantial records of man's broad social and moral experience; they are seriously conceived and carefully wrought artistic statements about observable life.

Blease, W. L. *The Emancipation of English Women.* London: Constable & Company, 1910. Though an older study, Blease succinctly describes the state and fate of the subjugated, imprisoned woman of the eighteenth century; the basis of their training, he notes, was sexual, and the role they are asked to fulfill is that of sexual plaything to the controlling male.

Brissenden, R. F. *Virtue in Distress: Studies in the Novel of Sentiment from Richardson to Sade.* New York: Barnes & Noble, 1974. Brissenden traces the ubiquitous nature of the theme of persecuted innocence in the novel beginning with Richardson's *Pamela.*

Clark, Alice. *Working Life of Women in the Seventeenth Century*. London: Routledge & Kegan Paul, 1919. In the belief that the conditions under which the obscure mass of women live and fulfill their duties as human beings has a vital influence upon the destinies of the human race, Clark investigates woman's role in agriculture, textiles, crafts, and trade, and the professions of nursing and midwifery. Excellent background material.

Day, Robert Adams. *Told in Letters: Epistolary Fiction Before Richardson*. Ann Arbor: University of Michigan Press, 1966. Day traces the history and methods of using letters to tell a story with over 200 little-known works preceding *Pamela*. In particular, he presents the Grub Street world that gave rise to such novelists as Haywood.

Dollard, John et al. *Frustration and Aggression*. New Haven: Yale University Press, 1939. Dollard presents a classic study of the role that frustration and aggression play in the inner life of people. The work is important because it reveals the inner motivation of such writers as Haywood and explores her interior rage and frustration.

Doody, Margaret Anne. "Deserts, Ruins and Troubled Waters: Female Dreams in Fiction and the Development of the Gothic Novel," *Genre*, 10 (1977):529–72. Dreams, as told in fiction, reveal inner terrors; women who dream in eighteenth-century fiction are depicted as living an inward life very different from their exterior one and from that of men. Through dreams, the novelists reveal the psyche of their feminine characters.

Foster, James R. *The History of the Pre-Romantic Novel in England*. New York: Modern Language Association, 1949. Foster investigates the notion of sensibility as it appears in early novels. He studies many of the minor figures of the eighteenth century.

Fritz, Paul, and Richard Morton (eds.). *Woman in the 18th Century and Other Essays*. Toronto: A. M. Hakkert, 1976. An excellent collection of essays about the women novelists of the period. Although none of the essays focuses on Haywood, they are useful for background information.

Fussell, Paul. *The Rhetorical World of Angustan Humanism*. New York: Oxford University Press, 1965. Excellent background material. Fussell studies the "humanist conception of man" as it appears in the major works of eighteenth-century literature.

George, M. Dorothy. *London Life in the Eighteenth Century*. New York: Harper & Row, 1964. Excellent study of housing, living conditions, disease rate, mortality rate, and so forth in London, circa 1700–1815. Useful as background source.

Greenberg, Janelle. "The Legal Status of the English Woman in Early Eighteenth-Century Common Law and Equity." *Studies in Eighteenth-*

Century Culture, ed. Harold E. Pagliaro, 4 (1974):171–82. Concise explanation of the legal status of the average eighteenth-century woman; excellent.

Greene, Donald. *The Age of Exuberance: Backgrounds to Eighteenth-Century English Literature.* New York: Random House, 1970. Basic background information emphasizing the vitality and energy of the age.

Horner, Joyce M. "The English Women Novelists and Their Connection with the Feminist Movement (1688–1897)," *Smith College Studies in Modern Languages,* 11, nos. 1–3 (October 1929, January and April 1930):1–152. One of the few critical studies of early eighteenth-century women novelists; because her scope is so vast, each novelist is treated in a cursory fashion; however, it is useful for the information that she does give.

Kamm, Josephine. *Hope Deferred. Girls' Education in English History.* London: Methuen, 1965. Good historical study of exactly what English girls were taught; useful as background material.

Koon, Helene. "Eliza Haywood and the *Female Spectator,*" *Huntington Library Quarterly,* 42 (1978):43–55. One of two published articles dealing with Haywood's work. Koon's study of the *Female Spectator* is important because this was the first magazine by and for women.

McBurney, William Harlin. "Mrs. Penelope Aubin and the Early Eighteenth-Century English Novel," *Huntington Library Quarterly,* 20 (May 1957):245–67. McBurney's article is important for the facts he reveals about eighteenth-century fiction before Richardson. Although mainly concerned with the pious polemics of Mrs. Aubin, he does glance at the early Haywood novels.

MacCarthy, Bridget G. *Women Writers: Their Contributions to the English Novel, 1621–1744.* New York: William Salloch, 1948. One of the few critical books to investigate the woman question and the woman novelist; because MacCarthy provides a survey, she is not able to make more than mundane observations about the numerous women writers.

Miller, Nancy. "Emphasis Added: Plots and Plausibilities in Women's Fiction," *PMLA,* 96 (January 1981):36–47. Miller explores women's fiction and finds that the writers adopt a "posture of imposture" that allows them to present their "true" story—the tale of exploitation and subjection—under the cover of an acceptable fiction.

Mish, Charles E. "English Short Fiction in the Seventeenth Century," *Studies in Short Fiction,* 6 (1968–1969):233–330. Good source for plots and influences of continental romances on early British fiction.

Morgan, Charlotte E. *The Rise of the Novel of Manners: A Study of English Prose Fiction Between 1600 and 1740.* New York: Columbia University Press, 1911. Although dated, this is a classic study of early feminine fiction. Morgan is one of the few critics to be aware of Haywood and to evaluate carefully her prose fictions.

O'Malley, I. B. *Woman in Subjection. A Study of the Lives of English Women Before 1832.* London: Duckworth, 1933. Together with Blease's book, O'Malley provides necessary background information on the plight of women during the eighteenth century.

Richetti, John J. *Popular Fiction Before Richardson: Narrative Patterns 1700–1739.* Oxford: Clarendon Press, 1969. An excellent study of the rogue, travel, pious polemic, scandal chronicles, and romances of the early period of British fiction. Richetti devotes a large amount of space to analyzing what he considers Haywood's demi-pornography.

Schofield, Mary Anne. *Quiet Rebellion: The Fictional Heroines of Eliza Haywood.* Washington: University Press of America, 1981. A study of Haywood's characters as spokeswomen for her gospel of revolution.

Showalter, Elaine. *A Literature of Their Own. British Women Novelists from Brontë to Lessing.* Princeton, N.J.: Princeton University Press, 1977. Initial chapters are invaluable for presenting the case for feminine literature; Showalter investigates the "female tradition" and the female novelist's "will to write."

Spacks, Patricia Meyer. "Early Fiction and the Frightened Male," *Novel: A Forum on Fiction,* 9 (1974–1975):5–15. The early fiction delineates a power struggle as the novels concern themselves with money, families, bodies, feelings. Sex and sexual relationships become the prime focus of the early fiction, and Spacks reveals the inherent fear the male has about the suddenly very sexually potent female.

————. "Ev'ry Woman is at Heart a Rake," *Eighteenth-Century Studies,* 8 (1974–1975):27–46. A woman, Spacks observes, has virtually no freedom of emotional expression; the patterns and concerns displayed in eighteenth-century fiction—obsession with innocence, anger at men, longing to be a man or a child—emphasize this lack of freedom. Spacks investigates these patterns.

————. *Imagining a Self: Autobiography and Novel in Eighteenth-Century England.* Cambridge: Harvard University Press, 1976. Spacks explores the affinities between the novel and the memoir. Chapter 3, "Female Identities," is especially pertinent to this study of Haywood.

Steeves, Harrison R. *Before Jane Austen: The Shaping of the English Novel in the Eighteenth Century.* London: George Allen & Unwin, 1965. Vintage study of the male reading of early eighteenth-century women's novels.

Stone, Lawrence. *The Family, Sex, and Marriage in England 1500–1800.* New York: Harper & Row, 1977. Excellent sociological study of family and living patterns during the early centuries of British fiction.

Stone studies family evolution, the role of the parents, fathers, daughters, and so forth. Invaluable charts and figures.

Watson, Barbara Bellow. "On Power and the Literary Text," *Signs,* 1 (1975–1976):111–18. In their fictions, women study the abuse of power to which they are subjected; they quickly learn to hide their real feelings and their show of power underneath male-approved pretense.

Watt, Ian. *The Rise of the Novel: Studies in Defoe, Richardson and Fielding.* Berkeley: University of California Press, 1957. Definitive study of the early eighteenth-century reading public.

Whicher, George Frisbie. *The Life and Romances of Mrs. Eliza Haywood.* New York: Columbia Univiersity Press, 1915. Until recently, the only published work on Eliza Haywood. Whicher combines the critical examination with biographical reporting.

Index